MW00912844

shadows in cages
Mothers and Children in Indian Prisons

shadows in cages
Mothers and Children in Indian Prisons

Ruzbeh Nari Bharucha

HIMALAYAN INSTITUTE®
PRESS
HONESDALE, PA 18431 USA

Himalayan Institute Press
952 Bethany Turnpike
Honesdale, PA 18431

www.HimalayanInstitute.org
©2004 by Ruzbeh Nari Bharucha

10 09 08 07 06
6 5 4 3 2 1

All rights reserved. No part of this book in any manner, in whole or in part, in English or in any other language, may be reproduced or transmitted in any form or by any means, electronic or mechanical, including photocopying and recording, or by any information storage or retrieval system without prior written permission of the copyright owner.

Published by the Himalayan International Institute Press of Yoga Science and Philosophy, 2006.
Originally published by Fusion Books, 2004.
Printed in Malaysia.

The paper used in this publication meets the minimum requirements of American National Standard for Information Sciences—Permanence of Paper for Printed Library Materials, ANSI Z39.48-1984.

Bharucha, Ruzbeh Nari.
Shadows in cages: mothers and children in Indian prisons / Ruzbeh Nari Bharucha.
    p. cm.
Reprint. Originally published: New Delhi : Fusion Books, 2004.
Summary: "Reveals the prison conditions in India for women inmates and their children and explores the obstacles they must overcome. Filled with personal interviews from the inmates and a candid look at a system that is greatly in need of reform"—Provided by publisher.
Includes bibliographical references and index.
    ISBN-13: 978-0-89389-259-3 (alk. paper)
    ISBN-10: 0-89389-259-9 (alk. paper)
    1. Women prisoners—India—Social conditions—Case studies.
    2. Children of women prisoners—India—Social conditions—
Case studies. I. Title.
    HV9793.B43 2006
    365'.60820954—dc22   2005035634

If any one of you is without sin,
let him be the first to throw a stone.

—John 8:7

table of contents

Jai Baba

To my children, as and when you remember,
and to my children in prison, if and when you forget.

THE DALAI LAMA

foreword

Traditionally, the world over, a mother and child are regarded as a symbol of kindness, care, and protection. This book focuses, however, on the plight of neglected and often forgotten mothers who find themselves in Indian prisons, many not even convicted but merely awaiting trial. Although these imprisoned women may keep their children under five with them, they are parted from the older ones and are themselves deprived of the kindness, care, and protection they would ordinarily expect of their families. Fortunately, there are NGOs to help and support them that I believe are doing important work.

Whatever they may have done or are accused of doing, these women remain human beings like the rest of us, concerned for their families and children and seeking affection and solace themselves. Kindness and compassion are extremely important in every area of life, whether it involves prisoners, prison guards, or victims of crime. While harboring hatred and ill will is futile, fostering cooperation, trust, and consideration is far more constructive. This is why I believe that those who give their time and energy humanely in the service of others, such as these imprisoned women, are worthy of our admiration and support. Such generosity represents a somewhat higher order of giving, for the most compassionate form of giving is when it is done without any thought or expectation of reward, and grounded in genuine concern for others.

Clearly, the work of organizations like the India Vision Foundation, in attempting to address real problems associated with prison life in India, is very important to everyone concerned. I hope that this book, *Shadows in Cages,* will inspire more individuals to help others in trouble who can no longer easily help themselves.

His Holiness the Dalai Lama

The names of the mothers and children
have been changed for purposes of privacy.

why this book?

In early 1994, as the editor of the *Pune Tribune*, I read a press clipping about mothers and their children in Pune's Yerwada prison. At first I thought it was a printing error. I couldn't believe that children were imprisoned and had to obey all the rules and regulations applicable to their imprisoned mothers. But what really disturbed me was realizing that after they reached the age of five, they were separated from their mothers and put into government-run orphanages. The thought of mother and child, after spending five intimate years of day and night together and then being separated maybe forever, affected my very soul.

Life moved on. Sometimes the image of mother and child in prison would surface in my mind for a fleeting moment, only to be wiped out by the demands of daily life. Nevertheless, my mind kept drifting back to that news clipping. Obviously, somewhere in the soil of my subconscious, the seeds for this book and a documentary on women in prison had been sowed. I assumed that by writing this book and directing the film, the image of that mother and child would be exorcised. I couldn't have been more wrong. It has been a long journey, but something tells me that it has only just begun. I hope this journey—the desire to make a difference no matter what—begins for you, too.

Ruzbeh Nari Bharucha

family life behind bars

THE WOMEN'S SECTION of the Yerwada jail is across the road from the main prison. You enter through a massive iron gate. On the left the visiting room is sandwiched between the front gate and the main gate. On the right is the office of the head jailor, a position held by Madam Pallavi Kadam. I meet her here in the morning before my interviews with the inmates. Her office is small but airy and well lit. As I wait for my interviews to begin, I look around and notice a framed photograph of Sai Baba of Shirdi (a saint much loved all over India). Above my head hang three large paintings of various famous Maratha women. In the corner next to my chair, I see two kittens, both asleep.

"They are not even a week old," says Madam Kadam.

"Where's their mother?"

"Roaming about. She should return now to feed them. You want them? You can have them." She smiles.

"Tell me, how many women prisoners are there in Yerwada?"

"At the moment there are 271 inmates."

"Have they all been convicted?"

"No. Many are waiting for trials."

"What is the capacity of the women's jail?"

She smiles, picks up a pen, and answers as diplomatically as possible, "You know, in most prisons, space is the main problem."

"Yes, so I have been told. But what is the capacity of this prison?"

"The real capacity is 126."

"You mean at the moment you have 145 extra inmates?"

"Yes. One of the major problems in most jails is overcrowding. There are times we have had to manage 300."

"That must be hell for the inmates!" I exclaimed. She nodded.

"Do the mothers with children in the prison live in a different quarter, or are they held with the rest?" I asked.

"Mr. Bharucha, there is no space to allow such differentiation. I wish we could put mothers and children in a separate quarter, but unfortunately it is not possible."

The phone rang. I watched the kittens. My thoughts drifted to the children who lived day after day in those overcrowded cells. The normal capacity was barely 32 inmates per cell. On an average day, there were at least 68 inmates crammed together, and on an exceptionally bad day, one cell could have up to 75 inmates living together. Madam Kadam finished her conversation on the phone and turned to me again.

"There must be a lot of fighting in these cells because of space constraints."

"Sometimes. But mostly the women live or try to live as peacefully as possible. Yes, there is very little space for sleeping, and most trouble originates because of this problem."

The phone shrilled once again. I remembered reading an interview with the editor of a Marathi newspaper who went to prison for just a day. The prisoners in Arthur Road jail told him that during the night, due to lack of space, the inmates had to take turns sleeping. So while a few slept, their cell-brothers stood.

"How many fans are installed in each quarter?" I inquired.

"No fans are allowed in prisons."

"You must be joking. Pune is extremely hot in the summer. How can so many prisoners, crammed into one small cell, live under one roof without fans? It is inhuman!" I lived in Pune during the summer. The heat makes the body virtually ache. You feel pressure-cooked, even with a fan operating at full speed. To have 70 inmates living in one cell all summer without a fan was appalling.

"Fans are not allowed in Yerwada prison, Mr. Bharucha."

"Wait a minute. You think somebody will use a fan to commit suicide?"

"Laws have been laid down. We just follow them."

I think this law was made by people with their bellies full, seated in comfortable and opulent surroundings. Let them spend a few days in the thick of summer in an over-crowded cell, and I have a strong feeling that certain laws will be modified with amazing alacrity.

"Tell me, are the ceilings of these cells low?" I asked.

"No. The ceilings are high."

"So, the law thinks that a few like-minded individuals will form a human pyramid to help a fellow inmate commit suicide by hanging from the ceiling fan? That's ridiculous!"

"Mr. Bharucha, I don't know. We just follow the rules and regulations. I know it does get hot in the cells during the summer, but there are huge windows and the door is massive, like a huge gate, and it allows ventilation. And remember, in both wings of Yerwada jail there are ample trees that give shade and protection from the glare of the sun. Other jails are, of course . . ." She did not have to complete the sentence. It is common knowledge that there are certain prisons in India that can compete with Lucifer's hell.

Yes, where Yerwada was concerned, I had seen enough from the inner main gate to realize that this jail at least tried to treat the inmates like human beings. They lived in a jail, but at least it looked like a garden—a caged garden.

"At what time are they locked in for the night?"

"By about 5:30 in the evening all the prisoners and children must be in their cell for the night."

"You mean even children are all locked up in this over-crowded cell by 5:30? Isn't that a little too early?"

"Yes, it is early, but all the inmates have to be accounted for and this has to be done in daylight."

"Are they allowed to come out for dinner?"

"No. They are given their dinner by 5:00 at the latest. If that's too early, they can take the food and eat it later."

Cold jail food. That's food for thought. I turned and looked at the kittens who were now contentedly nursing.

Please Help Me Find My Son

It was time for my interviews. The visiting room is divided into two sections separated by grills. One side is for the prisoners, the other for their visitors. It was a dark, dismal room, certainly not conducive to meeting loved ones after months of longing and separation. Fortunately, Madam Kadam has allowed the women and children to sit and talk to me in the visitors' section. The children are happy to be on the other side of the fence. Shenaz Sheikh, a social worker representing an NGO (non-government organization) called Saathi, has made all the arrangements, and introduced me first to Radha.

"For God's sake, please help me find my son." Tears rolled down Radha's sunken cheeks. The child prancing around her became still. Her small fingers caressed her mother's face. Radha wiped away her tears and then took her little girl on her lap.

The prison guard looked on sympathetically. God knows how many tears she had witnessed through the years. It was a wonder that she still had compassion in her eyes. She tickled the child, who was torn between her desire to explore this new room and the need to be near her mother.

"Go play." Saying this, Radha tenderly put the child down from her lap. She looked at me and then lowered her gaze. "She misses her brother so much. We haven't seen him for two years. She cries for her brother nearly every day."

"But why hasn't he been brought here to see you?" I asked.

Shenaz explained, "We have tried hard. We have tried every possible means. Even the jailor has written letters to the government orphanage asking that the son be brought to see his mother, but there still has been no response."

"I don't understand. Isn't there a law that makes it compulsory for social institutions that keep prisoners' children to make certain that the mother and child meet every few months, if not every month?"

"No. You must understand that these institutions have their own problems. Often, they are short of cash and short of staff. Part of the problem is that these institutions are outside the city. They could be hours from the prison in which the mother is being kept."

"That is understandable, but shouldn't children be put in orphanages that are within the city in which the mother is imprisoned?"

"Logically, that would be the policy."

"But there is no law enforcing it."

"No, there is no such law." Shenaz looked resigned. It was obvious that the suffering and frustration that she faced every day working with the inmates at Yerwada jail had left a deep mark on her psyche.

I struggled to keep the words flowing. This is a Marathi-speaking population, and at best I dished out a confusing concoction of Marathi, Hindi, Gujarati, and English.

"How old is your son?" I asked Radha.

"Seven."

"You had both children with you in prison, but when your son reached the age of five, he was sent to a government orphanage, and you haven't seen him since then?"

"Yes." She nodded, and once again the tears flowed. It is depressing and heartwrenching to see such pain. I took a deep breath.

"Have you asked the authorities to help?"

Shenaz spoke up. "Normally we write a letter on behalf of the mother, who is frequently illiterate. If we get no response, then we write the letter through our organization, Saathi. If the response is still not favorable, or the child still has not seen his mother, then Madam Kadam, the jailor, writes the letter."

"Where is the child?"

"In Kolhapur." Kolhapur is only a few hours' journey by bus.

"But if the mother and child still have not met in a case like this, don't you think the mother or your social organization can ask the court to intervene and order the child to be brought to his mother?"

"There is no law that can force an organization to bring the child to meet the mother in prison. You must remember that they are doing their best under the circumstances. They are really short of cash and staff."

"Yes, but you can't keep a mother from seeing her child for two years! I mean, this is not morally right! There should be some provision made, and if the State has placed the child so far away, then the State should foot the bill to let mother and child meet. Why is the child not kept in an institution in Pune?"

"The children are transferred from place to place for various reasons. Sometimes all the institutions in the city are already packed to capacity. At other times, the child is sent to a particular institution with the assumption that the child might learn a craft taught only there," Shenaz explained.

Again tears rolled down Radha's face. "I have not seen my son for such a long time that I'm not sure whether he will even remember me."

"Let me see if I can find your son. I don't know how, but I will try my best."

She nodded and left. I suspect she really wanted to believe me, but no doubt I am not the first person to promise help and then disappear.

Born in Prison

I was exhausted. I hadn't been in that dingy, dour room more than fifteen minutes, and still I felt every last ounce of strength within me drained by the cumulative misery of all the prisoners who must have used this room to meet with their loved ones.

Shenaz appeared again. "The next prisoner you'll meet is here for life. She killed her husband. She has a five-year-old girl who will be sent to a government orphanage the day after tomorrow. The little girl was born here in the prison."

I sighed. I could not begin to imagine what this mother must be going through. Just a day left to spend with her daughter, and then, in all probability, she'd lose the child forever to a bunch of strangers. It must be heartbreaking, especially when she and her child have spent five years with each other day and night in such an intense environment.

What does it feel like to have a piece of your heart torn out forever? To realize that you will never again be there when your child cries out for you, never again nurse her through a raging fever, and never again wipe away her tears? With luck, she might see her child for an hour or two once a month, otherwise, perhaps not even once a year.

"This is Indrajit Singh and this is her daughter, Geeta," said Shenaz.

A white sari covered Indrajit's body, and a masklike face, devoid of emotion, concealed her state of mind. I could not gauge her age. She could have been in her twenties or even in her forties. She looked at me and then folded her hands into *namaste,* a gesture of respect. I reciprocated.

Geeta was a sprightly young girl with a round face, chubby cheeks, and eyes that twinkled with laughter. In fact, upon meeting the children in Yerwada, it was obvious that they were well cared for. Even the clothes the children wore were well maintained and the joie de vivre in their body language was palpable and heartening.

"Say hello," Indrajit coaxed the child who was staring at me as though I had just stepped out of a spaceship. She was perplexed. No doubt she had rarely met men and did not know what to expect of me. Like a mature, good citizen of this great land of ours, I did the only responsible thing that came to mind—I winked at her. Like the sun peeping out from a cloud, a smile appeared on the child's face.

"She has been told that she is going for an outing day after tomorrow, so she is excited," Shenaz explained in English.

My heart cringed. I found it difficult to meet Geeta's open and honest eyes. It was a dismal, heartbreaking scene that came to mind. How long would it take this happy little girl to realize that she was never going back to live with her mother? That her mother, in all probability, would never lull her to sleep again; that the soft voice of her mother, coaxing her to eat or sleep or behave herself, would be replaced by the voices of strangers? How would the foster guardians explain to this five-year-old girl that, through no fault of her own, she too faced imprisonment of a different kind? She would no longer have her mother to protect, tend, play with, hug, and comfort her. Her entire life was going to turn upside down within forty-eight hours. I could not look into Geeta's trusting eyes.

"Come on, Geeta, recite that new poem the teacher taught you."

Geeta jumped down from her mother's lap and stood at

attention. At first she was shy, but when I smiled, her eyes lit up, and she took a deep breath and began. As she narrated the poem about a child's love for her mother, Geeta's mother began to cry. Tears rolled down her face and she shut her eyes. The poem told of a child's love and need for her mother, and the mother's selfless love for her child. It explained how the child need never worry, for God had created mothers because he could not be everywhere at the same time.

As she continued the narration, I wondered why this child had been taught this poem. Her little heart would be broken in two days, and as mothers could not be everywhere, I fervently hoped and prayed that the good Lord would be there when these children of his would need his loving care and tenderness.

". . . and every night my mother holds me tight, till I enter the world of paradise." She finished and then looked at me shyly and hid her face in her mother's lap.

I asked Indrajit if she had other children.

"Geeta is her lover's child," offered Shenaz.

"Pardon me?"

"Her lover's child," Shenaz explained in English. "She has four children from her first marriage. Her lover is a Maratha, but she is a Sikh. She had run away with her lover, who used to work for her husband. She and her lover killed her husband. They were convicted of the crime and sentenced to life in prison. According to Indrajit, her brother-in-law killed her husband. But that is her version. God alone knows what really happened."

"What about the four children from her first marriage?"

"They have never come to see her. They are being looked after by her in-laws."

"You mean she has not seen her children since she was imprisoned?"

"For five years there has not been even a letter to her."

"Where is her lover?"

"In the main Yerwada prison across the road."

I turned to face the woman who had supposedly killed her husband and orphaned her four children. All I saw was a woman scared for her little girl, who would be separated from her within forty-eight hours. Even if she had killed her husband, there was no trace of a murderer in her demeanor. Just a defeated mother, looking at me pleadingly.

"Does your child see her father?"

"Yes. As none of the family come to see us, we are allowed to see him once a month. She loves him very much."

Tears slowly trickled down her cheeks. "Neither of us knows how to live without her."

I wanted to ask about her other four children, but the surroundings, the lack of privacy, and the language barriers all got in the way.

"Isn't there anyone who could take care of her?"

"As far as my family is concerned, I am dead."

At the door Geeta giggled and ran to her mother's arms.

"I don't know how I will live without her," she said again.

The guard patted the grieving mother. "It is best for her, Indrajit. You know that. It is better for your child that she spends her life in a good institution than in a prison."

Indrajit nodded in agreement and wiped away her tears.

"I know, but who will take care of her?"

"They will take care of her, and teach her, and make her clever, so that she grows up to be a successful woman. Right, Geeta?"

The little girl nodded, but in her eyes was a sudden fear. She didn't understand the tears and the anguish. She had been told she was going to a new school for a day. No need to cry over such a wonderful outing. Perhaps instinct warned her that something was amiss. Her mother hugged her.

"Can I visit her once she is in the institution?" I inquired. "Will you? Please?"

"Yes, I will. Shenaz will take me there."

Geeta looked me in the eye with a thousand-watt smile. I tried my best to meet her gaze.

A Life Sentence and a Five-Year-Old

My third interview in the Yerwada jail was with Rehana. A young boy of five came with her. He held his mother's hand tightly.

"This is Rehana. She is in for life." Shenaz made the introductions.

"Don't tell me she also killed her husband?" I inquired in English.

"No. She was involved in a fight with another woman who died. It seems there was a fight over water. In poor localities water is not readily available. The women have to wait in line to fill their buckets with water. She and a friend had a fight with another woman. That woman, in sheer frustration, poured kerosene over herself and set herself on fire. Rehana and her friend were imprisoned. Her friend died recently of AIDS."

I sighed. A woman had burned herself to death, and another woman was in prison for life over scarcity of water. Actually it's not really a scarcity of water. Many people are too poor to afford a proper water connection, or they are illegal tenants who are not entitled to a legal connection and who can't afford an expensive illegal connection. In a few days India would celebrate her fifty-fifth year of independence. I wondered what Mahatma Gandhi and all those innumerable brave freedom fighters who sacrificed their youth, their families and their lives would say about the plight of our brethren.

"What's your name?" I asked the young boy staring at me with conflicting emotions in his big eyes. I did not blame him for his obvious confusion. Men are not allowed in the Yerwada jail. On the rare occasion when a man is given permission to enter, it is usually the police, or a social worker, or a doctor. The visit is brief and impersonal. Thus, for most children, communication with men is rare.

"Tell him your name, son," his mother urged. A blush spread over the child's face.

"Maybe he has forgotten his name." I smiled.

"No. I know my name. My name is Shyam."

"Lovely name." I patted his head and he beamed.

"How long has he been with you?" I asked Rehana.

"He was born here." Shyam moved toward the door.

"Have you told him about . . . uh . . . his leaving . . . ?" I could not complete the question. Tears ran down her face. She shook her head.

"Actually, she has a daughter, also, who is living with her husband," Shenaz added.

"Why can't he keep Shyam, too?"

"The problem is that he has not responded to any of our letters for the last six months."

"Are you sure he has received the letters? What if he hasn't got them? When was the last time he visited his wife and child?"

"Around six to seven months ago. He wasn't well and had not been well for a long time." Shenaz switched to English. "We don't know whether or not he is alive. Also, he is a Sindhi and she is a Muslim, so I suspect his family are not very accepting of her or her child."

"Can't you send somebody to check on him? Where does he live?"

"Who will go?"

"Isn't there some kind of law that makes it mandatory

for the State to contact the father before the child is put in an institution?"

"No such law exists."

"Then why can't a social organization take this responsibility?"

"Most social organizations are already . . ."

"Yeah, yeah, I know, I know. Cash and staff starved."

"Yes. We try our best, but often the best is not good enough."

I turned back to Rehana.

"Where does your husband live?"

"Manmad, near Nasik. It is only seven hours from here."

"Okay. I am going to Nasik one of these days."

"Will you please go and see my husband and daughter? Please find out how they are and why no one has written or visited me. Please!"

"I will go, but tell me, Shenaz, why can't somebody from the Nasik prison send the police to see whether the father is ready to take care of his son or wants the child sent to an orphanage?"

"It doesn't work like that."

"Okay. Forget the police. Why can't a social organization working in Nasik find out why the man is not answering any letters."

"As I said, most organizations are already short of staff."

It was frustrating. Here is a child who could possibly be reunited with his father and live in his own home, but instead would be sent to an orphanage.

"Whenever you go to Nasik, I would be really grateful if you could go visit my daughter and husband," Rehana pleaded.

I nodded and stood up. Shyam held his mother's hand and looked up at me. He was not certain whether to smile or just go away. I caressed his head and he smiled. There was silence for a while. Then they left and Shenaz introduced the next prisoner.

Nobody Wants Us

"The lady coming in is Shardabai Sathey."

I nodded and waited to hear another gut-wrenching story. I did not have the heart to ask why she was in prison.

Shenaz told me anyway. "In sheer frustration she threw her child down a well. The baby died and she has been convicted of murder."

Shardabai Sathey came in with her five-year-old daughter tightly clutching her mother's hand. What must it be like to spend nearly five years in a closed cell, day in and day out, remembering how in sheer anger and frustration you had killed your own child? One does not have to die to go to hell. Hell is right here—in our hearts and minds. What could have driven this woman to kill her own child? Poverty, hunger, abuse—what kind of madness could have propelled a mother to lash out at the most innocent of her loved ones?

Shardabai's face was a mask. Her eyes gave away little. All through the conversation she expressed no emotion. Only when she looked at her daughter, Neerja, did tenderness enter her eyes. The young girl was a sprightly, happy child. It was obvious that she was oblivious to her mother's past and her own future. In two days, she too would be separated from her mother. Neerja played near the entrance and for a while we were silent.

"Isn't there anybody in the family who can look after Neerja?"

"Nobody wants us. Nobody has come to see either me or her."

"What about your parents?"

"To my husband and my parents, I am dead and so is my daughter." She spoke in a soft but detached tone, as though five years in prison had been a slow but sure teacher. Either she was totally detached or totally repressed.

"We do not even know where her husband lives. He just left for some other place," Shenaz explained. I did not blame him. A man can go mad knowing that his own wife has taken the life of their child.

I couldn't ask her any questions. What does one ask? Why did you kill your child? How do you feel about it? Are you repentant? We spoke about Neerja and it was obvious that the separation was eating into the mother's heart, but she did not show any emotion. She stood up, stared into my eyes, and left.

"I want you to meet just one more inmate. The last one of the day." Saying this, Shenaz left the room. My mind drifted to all that had resulted in my being here in the first place. Outside the gate I could hear a bird screaming. Somewhere a vehicle zoomed by. I could not see any of this world, but I could hear it, just like the women imprisoned here. Freedom is the most underrated of all the gifts God has given us.

I looked around. I was still seated in the dingy visitors' room. It was stuffy within these walls, and I wondered how the children lived, day in and day out, in a cell that had no fan and was forever overcrowded. All this talk about ventilation and trees and gardens sounds nice, but in a country like India, where the summer heat is deadly, being herded into an overcrowded room without fans and basic necessities is cruel and inhuman. It seemed to me that instead of reforming prisoners, our authorities are only making them more negative and filled with hatred. Don't we imprison people with the hope that they will reform themselves and return to society as law-abiding citizens? If imprisonment breeds anger and hatred, these people are more dangerous when they leave than when they entered prison.

Our Letters Go Unanswered

Shenaz, the guard, and a middle-aged woman inmate entered the dismal room. I stood up and acknowledged the inmate's presence.

"This is Bharti," Shenaz said. "Tell Mr. Bharucha your problem."

Bharti's eyes spoke clearly of dark hours, pain, and tears. It was all so naked and raw that it unnerved me. One would have to be blind, preoccupied beyond words, or plainly daft to be unaffected by such raw emotions.

"My children are in a home in Raigad."

"On the road to Panchgani?"

"Yes." She began to weep. As though with a life of their own, tears streamed down her face. I remembered Raigad. From my lovely boarding school in Panchgani, I could see Raigad. It was on the other side of the mountain, across the valley.

"Don't cry. What is the matter?" I asked.

"Her children have not visited her for nearly two and a half years. They are in an institution and there has been no contact with them. Our letters go unanswered," Shenaz answered for her.

"How old are they?"

"My girl is thirteen and my son is eleven," Bharti sobbed.

I sighed. As a parent I can well understand how it must feel to have a thirteen-year-old girl at the mercy of the world. This poor woman lives each moment wondering about the welfare of her children. Imagine that your children are living with strangers and that you can't see them or talk to them. So you go on worrying for nearly three years. One does not necessarily need to die to experience hell.

"Please, son, just find out how they are," she begged with tears rolling down her face.

"I'll try my best," I assured her. It would take time, but I would try.

Interviews over, the women went back to their cells. I exhaled with sheer frustration and exhaustion. We live in paradise compared with these helpless women, whatever their crime. To live, dying each day, hoping and praying, and worse, waiting for one word from their children, falling asleep once again with only silence day after day, year after year—that is hell.

A Social Worker's View

A few days later, I was back in Pune. I had an appointment with Sanjeev, a social worker associated with Saathi. We met outside the Blue Diamond Hotel. During India's fight for independence, Sanjeev's grandfather, an engineer, owned a factory in a town near Pune. After a few years of financial success, he realized that despite being wealthy and having all the luxuries money could buy, he was still not happy. In fact, as years went by, the void within him grew only deeper.

In those days most Indians were trying their best to send the Britishers back to the Queen Mother, and the popularity of Gandhiji was at its peak. Sanjeev's grandfather decided to devote his life to something more than just earning lots of cash. He sold his factory, and, after providing for his family, he distributed a large chunk of the remaining amount to the poor and the needy. He also built an ashram in Madhan for underprivileged girls and needy women. He saw clearly that welfare activity was most needed in rural villages where more than 70 percent of India lived.

"Is the Madhan ashram still operative?" I asked.

"Yes, after my grandfather passed away, my grandmother ran the ashram, and now it is being looked after by other family members."

"How did you get involved in social work?"

As a young man, Sanjeev was not interested in social work or the ashram. In fact, until he was in the ninth grade, he had not even visited the ashram. Then, during one vacation, he was sent to visit his grandmother.

"I went to meet her and after that my life changed. I realized that if you have the intention, even one person can make so much difference in the lives of so many other people. After spending a few years as a social worker, I have come to the conclusion that each one of us can contribute in some way to make the life of others worth living. Also, by helping individuals you help society at large. For example, if a farmer is in trouble, he cannot farm properly. If you help just one farmer—and there are a thousand people like us helping different farmers in their own small way—then collectively you are helping society feed itself.

"I learned a lot from Anna Hazare (a renowned social worker in India). According to Annaji, if you concentrate social work activities in villages, you are helping India in a big way, since 70 percent of Indians live in rural areas. If the children in villages are educated and their foundation is strong, then you are building a great pillar for the future of our country."

"Was it this philosophy that inspired you to work for Saathi?"

"Yes. You see organizations like Saathi work for the

welfare of children whose mothers are in prison. Nearly 80 percent of these children are living in villages. Also, most organizations do not judge the child on the basis of the mother's crime. They want to help the children irrespective of the mother."

"What is your role?"

"My job is to ascertain whether the children of incarcerated mothers need help. Often the father is also not around. He has either deserted the family or is himself a criminal. The children are frequently in the care of their grandparents or other relatives," Sanjeev explained.

"How many such cases do you handle?"

"Around sixty children. I have been doing this type of work since 1997. As soon as a woman inmate is brought to Yerwada jail, somebody from Saathi records the details about the woman and her family and her background. We concentrate mainly on women with children. After the initial round of researching, I am given details like names, address, the number of children, where they are living and with whom. Then, I visit the place and see for myself how things stand and what kind of assistance can be given.

"For example, recently I investigated a case in a village near Sholapur. A six-year-old child was living with his grandmother about six kilometers from the bus stand. Usually, it is easy to locate the address of these children, as everyone knows in whose house the murder had taken place. So I was able to reach the place and found the child and the grandmother."

"Why was the child's mother in jail?" I asked.

"She killed her husband."

"There really are too many cases of the husband being murdered," I said.

"Yes. Usually they have abused their wives, their children, and everybody around them for years."

Wife abuse is very common. What usually happens is that one day the wife can take the abuse no longer and in sheer frustration and anger, she strikes the husband. The man is frequently already leading a dissolute life of drinking and indulgences, and he dies. Though the court may be sympathetic, it is bound by the law. Emotions cannot justify the action.

"This child was living with his father's mother. She told me that this child had the blood of her son, so she would take care of him as long as she lived."

"How old was she?"

"She was at least seventy years old. This poor old woman who had looked after her son and his family now had to work in the fields in order to take care of her grandson. Every morning she walked two kilometers to work and labored all day in the field for about 30 rupees (about 65 cents). Then, she would walk home, cook dinner, and feed the grandchild and herself."

"Who was taking care of the child?"

"The child was attending school and then would come home. In villages help comes from various sources." It takes a village to raise a child says the old African saying.

"My job in such a case is to ascertain whether or not the social organization should help this family. If we gave money, would it be spent on the child? In this case, obviously the money would be spent on the child, but there have been cases where the money was spent on liquor, for example, and so we had to withdraw help," Sanjeev told me.

"So you prepare a report and give suggestions."

"Yes. Once a month, we have a meeting and discuss each case. Then I make a report and give my recommendations. In this case I recommended that we help the child with whatever resources we had available, which turned out to be 200–250 rupees a month (US$5.00)."

It was unfortunate—an old woman, toiling for eight hours in the scorching sun or heavy rain, walking nearly four kilometers every day, then cooking and tending her grandchild and herself. Saathi had limited funds, and such cases were numerous. If individuals gave only a small part of their salaries—even 5 percent—to such organizations, so much help could reach the needy.

"Do you visit the children again?"

"Once I have submitted the report, my work is over, at least as far as that child is concerned. Someone else gives us information about the child when we need it. Usually the contact is the school. Normally, we grant money so that the education of the child does not suffer. If we are sending money and the child is not being sent to school, then we know there is something shady going on."

"How many years ago did you research the case you told me about?"

"Two years."

"Have you visited them again?"

"No, but as I told you, we get information from the school and other channels. The moment we feel that the money is used for activities other than the child's welfare, then I pay a visit. There have been times we have had to discontinue supporting a family. So I visit places again and again, if there's any doubt. There have been times when to the normal eye all is fine, but for the social worker, the body language of the child or the expression in the child's eyes tells a different story."

No doubt it is hard to keep a tab on each and every child who comes under the purview of a social organization. The reality of the situation is that most social organizations are in fact short staffed and short of cash. Given the circumstances, they were doing a remarkable job.

However, that does not change the grim reality of the children of prisoners. These are children without mothers, for all practical purposes, living with relatives, at the mercy of their kin who had their own families to look after. To add to the miserable situation, many, if not most, men drank themselves to ruin—the entire family's ruin.

"In your experience with these children, how do they cope without their mothers?" I pressed Sanjeev for answers.

"There are some children who just cannot cope with life without their mother. They are psychologically shattered and go on weeping and pining for her. But fortunately, most of the children adapt to the situation and live the best they possibly can under the circumstances. Friends, relatives, and new surroundings make a lot of difference. But there are some children who find it impossible to adjust to life without their mother. They write letters, and when I meet them, they ask for details about their mother, and are really disappointed when I cannot provide them with their mother's photograph."

"Don't they see their mothers?"

"Bharucha, they can't afford the trip."

"Isn't there any social organization that could provide transportation? How much can it cost? Not much, I am certain."

"There is no such organization, and don't you think that money could be better used for the children?"

"Do you have children of your own?"

"No."

"Then you won't understand the agony of not being able to see your child for months or even years. It is better to be dead than not to be able to take care of your child, or worse, not even to see or talk to your children for months on end," I said.

"Maybe. I have seen mothers in the jail who cry for

their children. They are really in a miserable state. Still, Bharucha, how many children will you be able to help meet with their mothers?"

"Let's take Yerwada jail or an organization that works with women inmates. How many mothers living in Yerwada jail have children living with relatives?" I asked.

"Say around a hundred at any given time. You know, it is a floating population. Women come and go and are transferred according to the court."

"Okay. Now tell me what is the cost for round-trip transportation to these villages?"

"On an average, a round trip would be about 200 rupees (US$4.50)."

"Okay, so for one person, the cost per day averages around 200 rupees. Add a child and the cost increases by another 100, since they are usually charged half a ticket; plus another 100 rupees or so for food," I calculated. "So assume the cost is around 400 or even 500 rupees for the relative to bring the child to visit his mother. That means around 50,000 rupees for a hundred children to meet their mothers. That means if a few people contribute just a few hundred rupees a year, such a trip could be sponsored. These children do not get to see their mothers for years, so even if we could manage to arrange trips twice a year, it would be a blessing for both the child and the mother. I think all it takes is a little caring from a larger section of society. I could easily set aside a percentage of income—just 1,000 rupees per year (US$20.00)—to help a child visit his mother."

"The concept is new, but I think it might work. But do you think it is really worth spending so much money to get mother and child together for just a day?"

"To let a child and mother visit, bond, and reassure themselves of each other's love and safety, it is definitely worth spending the money. I am sure it is worth much more!"

"Spending so much money for so short a visit really makes no sense." Sanjeev was not convinced.

"To really know whether it makes sense or not, Sanjeev, you must have a child. You must be a parent—and then you'll never ask such a question. I'd go mad if I was unable to visit my children. Every day these mothers must be dying inside, just because the family does not have a few hundred rupees to arrange the meeting. I think a social organization would be doing a really noble thing if at least once in six months they could let the children visit their mothers."

"You know," said Sanjeev, "the major problem is that these children are psychologically and emotionally maimed. However small the child is, he knows why his mother is in jail. Often relatives or friends or other children tell the child, 'Your mother is in jail for murder or robbery,' or whatever. Most children refuse to believe that their mother has committed any sort of crime. So, at an early age, the child spends time and energy justifying or denying the mother's actions."

"How is the judiciary in these cases? Are the judgments fair, pro-mother, or otherwise?"

"Bharucha, from the bottom of my heart, I wish that the judiciary was more fair. This is my opinion and doesn't reflect the social organization I represent. I have met so many children, and I estimate 70 percent of them have witnessed the murder or crime. In my opinion, in Yerwada jail alone, 90 percent of the judgments are not fair. This is my conclusion after four years of research."

"You mean, they've been imprisoned for the wrong reasons?"

"Wrong reasons? You'd be surprised. I'll give you an example. Once I had to visit a child living in a remote village. The bus stopped miles from my destination. It was after midnight, and I reached a temple at around two in the morning.

I stopped there for a few hours. At five in the morning, I again resumed my journey and met the child and the family. Then, during talks with them, it suddenly dawned on me that the child's mother, who was serving a twelve- or fifteen-year life sentence, had been a minor when she had committed the crime. She had been around sixteen or seventeen years old. The poor woman had already spent six years in prison. Nobody had bothered to inquire whether or not she was a minor when the crime was committed. She has been released now, but her entire youth was spent behind bars."

"Why did nobody notice this?"

"That is the strange part of this whole case. When the person is poor and illiterate, no one bothers to look into the details. This is the system in our country, where often even minors end up in jails, serving life sentences. I am not saying that every woman jailed is either a minor or innocent. There are times when a child will try to save his mother by insisting that she was not present during the crime, but often I feel that not enough attention is paid to the cases of poor people. This is my opinion."

"Has there been a case that has left a deep impression on you?"

"As a social worker, I need to keep my mind and heart detached from the things happening around me. Yes, it is hard, but I must, or lose my mental balance. I give time, effort, and my life for the welfare of people, but that does not mean I should allow their lives to affect me and overshadow everything around me. There are, of course, many times when their sorrow or courage touches me so deeply and profoundly that I also feel tears welling up in my eyes."

This is the reality of life. Social workers are doing their best, and often even the government is making an effort. But in a poor country where the average man does not get his share, to expect a prison inmate to get her rightful due and that which the constitution has promised her is asking for the moon.

For Lack of a Few Dollars

For a month, I was consumed with the logistics of daily life. I spent time working on the information I had already gathered and thought about spending a few more hours with the inmates. The plans for another trip to Yerwada brought about a strange sense of sadness. After every visit to the jail, I fell ill for a few days; and no doubt this fact contributed to the general sense of disquietude I felt upon my return.

Back in Madam Kadam's office, I was welcomed by the two kittens who were now nearly full grown. Shenaz sat nearby. Madam Kadam, after making the necessary arrangements for my interviews, left for other work. We decided to meet with the inmates in her office, rather than the claustrophobic visiting room. Shenaz introduced the first inmate.

"This is Geeta Rao."

A young woman walked in, accompanied by a child. It was hard to believe that just a few months earlier, she had allegedly killed her husband. During my last visit, we had decided to arrange bail money for her. Geeta, barely thirty years old, had three children, aged eight, six, and three.

"This is the same person who has organized your bail money," Shenaz told her. Both Geeta and I shifted uncomfortably in our seats.

"Are you being released on bail tomorrow?"

"Yes."

"Take care of your children."

"Yes, sahib."

I turned to Shenaz.

"How long will she be free on bail?"

"At least five to six years."

"Are you telling me that if we hadn't arranged for her bail money, she would have spent five or more years in prison, just waiting for trial, just waiting for her case to come up for a hearing?"

"Yes, that's right."

I looked at Geeta and then at her small child, who smiled shyly at me. I sighed. For want of 8,000 rupees (about US$170), an innocent mother may spend five years languishing in prison, wondering about the welfare of her children and dying inside a little each day.

"So, if inmates like her do not have bail money, they spend five or more years waiting for trial, and if found guilty, they are liable to be imprisoned for another God-knows-how-many years after that? This is an intolerable situation!"

"What to do? That is how the law works." Shenaz looked resigned.

"The law is wrong!"

"Bharucha, there are thousands waiting for trial who have spent years in prison because they did not have money for bail."

Imagine, even a person finally proven innocent may end up spending years in prison for want of a trifle amount—a sum that many spend on one dinner or on a new outfit. Either the government should provide justice within a few months or set bail that even the most humble of people can afford. If we believe "innocent until proven guilty," then how on earth can we lock away innocent people for years on end for want of a few thousand rupees?

"Who else lives at your home?" I asked Geeta.

"My mother, my younger brother and sister, and my two children."

"How old are your brother and sister?"

"My brother is twelve and my sister is fourteen."

"You must have married very young?"

"Very, very young." She blushed. Then she wept. Was it tears for all the dreams turned sour, for her dead husband, her abandoned children, for a life that could have been?

"Why did you kill him?"

She looked at me, not certain whether I would understand her state of mind or circumstances. In a manner of speaking, we came from two different universes. For a long time, she stared at me and then she said, "He used to beat me so badly. He would drink and abuse me. He never worked and would go on abusing me, and then he started abusing the children. One day I don't know what happened." Again tears rolled down her face. "My mother is a daily-wage earner. Thank God, I can go back and help her take care of my children and also my brother and sister." When she left, I looked out the window at the lovely garden where children were playing. There are so many women like her who need help. There is much that all of us can do. It just requires the right intention.

"How will social organizations help her further?" I asked Shenaz.

"A social worker will visit her home and assess the situation. We may find money for the education of her children."

"Is it 200 rupees (US$4.00) per child?"

"Yes."

I know 200 rupees is not much, but every rupee counts in the lives of these people. Much good comes from the most humble of intentions and contributions. Drop by drop, the ocean fills up.

My next interview was with Radha Karkar and her daughter, a six-year-old with lovely cheeks and big eyes, wearing false white pearls that matched her little white teeth. She stared at me in sheer wonderment.

"Another husband sent to play the harp?" I inquired in English.

"No. She and her husband and her brother are accused of killing another family."

This information took the wind out of me. I looked at the woman. I could see no cold-blooded murderer. Only a mother worried for the future of her child.

"They killed an entire family?"

"Four to five members of a family were killed. She denies it. She says she was not present when the murders took place."

Once again, I looked at her, and for the life of me I could not see a killer. At that moment, she looked like a woman who had gone through her own hell and did not need any further grief from the law.

I asked Shenaz why a six-year-old was still in the prison with her mother.

"Her case is about to come up. So we allowed the child to stay on until a verdict is given."

"How old was the child when her mother was imprisoned?"

"The mother was pregnant when she was taken into custody."

"You mean this woman has been in prison for six years and still hasn't been convicted?"

"Yes."

"She is here because she could not raise money for bail?"

"That's right."

"Sahib, I did not kill anybody," Radha spoke up.

I looked at her. If she had been part of the gory plan to wipe out a family, then she deserved what she was getting. But I shuddered to think of the other possibility—her innocence. What if she really was innocent? Six years in prison for being too poor to afford a few thousand rupees? And what about this little girl with fake pearls around her neck and the joy of youth in her eyes? Did this child deserve to spend the best years of childhood behind bars?

"Isn't there someone who can look after your daughter?" I asked Radha.

"My parents live in Osmanabad, but I am afraid to send her there," she replied.

Shenaz explained, "Her husband escaped from jail, and she is scared that he will take her daughter with him and disappear."

"If she is convicted, will the child be sent to a government orphanage?"

"Yes."

"Sahib, my husband has already threatened my parents. I can't let her stay with them. He will take her away. But I can take her and disappear so he can't find us. Please help me, sahib. Please." Having made her plea, she stood up to go, and Shenaz introduced the next woman.

"Deepa Patel is from Mumbai."

Deepa was apprehensive, but under the layers of fear and doubt was a glimpse of hope. I started to realize that most of these inmates survive on the hope for a miracle. She sat before me, clutching and twisting her fingers. She was a thin woman, like most of her sister inmates, eaten up by anger, doubt, sorrow, and hopelessness.

"Her case is slightly unusual," said Shenaz. "She divorced her husband nearly three years ago. A few months ago, her husband disappeared and then was found dead. She, her sister-in-law, and her sister's husband have been accused of this murder."

"Brother, I have done nothing. We were not even staying together. I had left my husband years ago. My ex-mother-in-law has done this to us. She wants my child and thus she planned the whole thing," Deepa explained.

"You mean your mother-in-law framed you?"

"Yes. I have not seen my husband for more than three years. I had nothing to do with him. He disappeared and died, and she told the police I was involved in his death. What would I get by his dying? She always hated me and now has put me in jail. She threatened my parents and took my child away."

"Why did the police believe her?"

"She has spent a lot of money." Though this was said clearly here in the office of the warden, no one was surprised, shocked, or even embarrassed.

"You are saying that she bribed the police?"

"Sahib, she is a horrible woman. She has taken all the children."

I looked first at Deepa and then at Shenaz. Obviously, I was missing something.

"The mother-in-law has all her grandchildren living with her," Shenaz explained. "Deepa's children, her sister's child, and the children of her sister-in-law."

"Sahib, she is a terrible woman. Please try to get me out of this place. I don't want anything but my child." She began to cry. I turned to Shenaz.

"If we manage bail for her, can she have custody of her child?"

"Yes."

"Can you promise that?"

"Yes. We can get a notice from the court that will force the mother-in-law to give Deepa custody of her child."

"Tell me why did the police believe the mother-in-law? Did you sign a document?" I asked Deepa.

"Yes, sahib. They forced us to sign papers."

"What do you mean, forced you to sign papers?"

"They beat us badly. We were in the lockup for nearly five days. They really beat us, sahib. One of them wore hard shoes and then stood on our feet to crush them."

"Which police station?"

"At Gamdevi, sahib. Then they moved us to Arthur Road jail. It is really terrible there. In a room for 50 women, there are 200." She began to weep again. "Sahib, please, I don't want anything. Just get me my child. That is all." Weeping, she folded her hands, stood up, and then, with head bent low and feeling defeated, she slowly left the room.

I wanted to leave, too. I don't know how to convey the tears, the anguish, the naked impotency, the frustration, and the emotional helplessness. I felt physically exhausted. It is no wonder that every time I visited jails and spoke to the inmates, I was ill for the next few days.

Next I met Deepa's sister-in-law, Meera, who has also been accused by the mother-in-law in the same case. Meera looked much like Deepa and narrated a similar story. Meera's daughter, Geeta, was eight years old. Three years earlier, the mother-in-law had been instrumental in kicking out the family, and she forcibly kept Meera's daughter. Now Meera's son had also been taken away from her. Naturally, the pain was visible in her eyes as well as in her body language.

Meera concurred with her sister-in-law's version of police brutality and confirmed that one officer had tried to crush their toes by stamping and standing on their feet with hard shoes. She left weeping.

"Do you think you can get bail money for them?" inquired Shenaz.

"I will try my best."

Two Years Without a Visit

I wondered how many such mothers were languishing in prisons all over the country—and all over the world.

I wondered how many could be reunited with their children. I looked at the framed photograph of Sai Baba on Madam Kadam's wall. He was smiling. God may be in heaven, but all was certainly not well in his world.

In walked yet another inmate. Her name was Poornima. She was young in years, but a hard life had prematurely aged her. The obvious signs of life in a state of perpetual conflict and agony were palpable in every movement and expression. A small child held her hand tightly. He was scared. Seeing so many strangers obviously unnerved him.

"She has been recently sentenced to life," Shenaz told me.

"How many years was she in jail awaiting trial?"

"Two years."

"How many children does she have?"

"Three outside of prison and one here."

I sighed. Two years in jail for want of money, while three children pined for their mother.

"How old are they?"

"The oldest brother is fourteen and the youngest, Rahul, is five."

"Where are your children staying at the moment?" I asked Poornima.

"All three are living with my husband's sister and family."

"Does she have children of her own?"

"Yes. Two children."

"Are they well off?"

"We send them 200 rupees per child," Shenaz explained.

I turned from Shenaz to Poornima.

"Do your children go to school?"

"Yes, they did. My daughter is in the eighth grade. But she does not go to school now. She wrote to me saying she wants to go to school, but my sister-in-law is not eager to send them to school anymore."

"When was the last time you had a visit with your children?"

"Two years ago. I have not seen them since I was imprisoned." Tears welled up in her eyes but she refused to cry, perhaps for the sake of her child.

"Please help me to see them. They miss me. They cry for me, but I cannot do anything for them. My daughter wrote to me that they are not sent to school and are not given proper clothes. I want them to go to a boarding school."

"Is that possible, Shenaz?"

"Yes it is. There are government boarding schools. They are not expensive, and they are decent."

"Then what in God's name are you waiting for?"

"*Bhai* [brother]," Poornima pleaded, "please help me to send them to a school. I want them to finish their schooling. My daughter wrote, 'Ma, they don't send us to school and we want to go.' Children don't lie, *bhai*. I want to see my children. Please do something." Then she wept. The child looked at his mother with big eyes, patted her hand, and caressed her face. She stood up and, without looking at us, left.

I shut my eyes and sighed.

"What would it cost for these children to see their mother?" I asked Shenaz.

"Three tickets for them, plus one for the adult who accompanies them. They live in Nagpur. I think 1,000 rupees (about US$20) should suffice."

For lack of 1,000 rupees, about what many of us spend on cigarettes or beer or amusement, a mother has not seen her three small children for more than two years.

"Can you get the children into a boarding school?"

"Yes," said Shenaz.

"First, we'll organize the trip."

The worst part of all of this is realizing that there are so many similar cases in the innumerable jails all over the country. I would not be able to do much for all of them.

But if there is anything I have learned, it is this: in our small way, even with humble means, we can make others' lives better.

All Poornima needed was a bit more than 1,000 rupees (US$20) to have her children visit. These are the children she had been unable to see for two years, all because she could not come up with the price of a T-shirt. If you are a parent, you can well imagine the daily anguish and tears she must have suffered. We arranged money for the visit—a total of 1,200 rupees. The three children visited their mother, and it was heartwrenching.

There are innumerable mothers in prisons who need such help. All it takes is a little effort and compassion on our part to bring a lot of solace and peace to the lives of hundreds of such mothers and thousands of such children. So many are languishing for years in jails waiting for trial because they are too poor to afford the bail. For want of a few thousand rupees, women spend years in jail, even before they have been proven guilty. This is an intolerable situation. There is much we can do, irrespective of how rich or poor we are. We can help bring light to many darkened lives.

A Visit to Rehana's Family

It was a trip long overdue. I had promised Rehana that I would inquire about the health and well-being of her husband and daughter. I intended to keep my word.

You will remember that Rehana is a Muslim woman married to a Sindhi (Hindu) man. She and her friend had a dispute with another woman over water. In this age of instant messaging and robots who do household work, women still stand in long lines every day for a few buckets of water for household use.

Unfortunately for Rehana, after the squabble, the other woman went home and committed suicide. Rehana and her friend (who later died in Yerwada jail with an AIDS-related disease) were locked up. If found guilty, she faces a life sentence. If found not guilty, due to her poverty, she has needlessly wasted five years of her life and youth in jail waiting for trial.

Rehana's son, Shyam, was at the moment in a government-run institute. Rehana was pregnant with Shyam when she was brought to Yerwada. Now Shyam is five years old and thus recently put into an institute that takes care of orphans and children of mothers who are in prison.

I wanted to see whether Rehana's husband was still alive. The last time he visited her he was very ill. Secondly, I wanted to inquire about their daughter, who had lived in Yerwada but at the age of five had been taken home by her father. The husband had not replied to the numerous letters sent by the authorities, Saathi, and his wife. Did he not want his son to live with him? Did he not want his children to live together? Was he still alive?

Rehana's Sindhi husband lived in a village near the city of Nasik in central India. In Nasik there is a consecrated place of worship that defies general norms. It was set up by so-called men of religion. This holy place was built in the memory of Meera Datta, a Sufi saint much revered by Muslims and Hindus alike. Mausoleums in his memory are found all through the country and are visited by those suffering from the evil forces of the spirit world (generally termed black magic). But in Nasik the difference was obvious and heartwarming. In this place of worship, Lord Shiva and Ganesh rub shoulders with Mecca and Medina. On one side are Vedic scriptures, and two feet away, a quote from the Koran proclaims, "Allah is the most merciful." Both Hindus and Muslims worship here.

The caretaker, my friend Madan's father-in-law, is a staunch Hindu who covers his head with a cloth, as all devout Muslims do, and, in the name of Meera Datta, prays for all those who come to this womb of religious and spiritual harmony. Before blessing all those who come seeking spiritual succor, the old man recites a verse from the Holy Koran, and then in the name of Meera Datta offers protection from any evil influence. A number of those possessed by negative spirits have been "cured" after coming to this spiritual power zone.

Madan had been a constant source of support. Whenever extra funding was required for mother-child inmates, he went out of his way to help. For instance, when Saathi needed sewing machines to help five women released from Yerwada start a small business to support themselves and their children, Madan sent the money to purchase the machines. Through those funds, five households had a means of survival. Again you see how we can help in our small ways to make a huge difference in the lives of these hapless mothers and children. I miss Madan and his soft voice and large heart!

After spending a wonderful day at this temple in Nasik, I took the train to the village of Manmad. The whole compartment was empty. I pinched myself to be sure that I was not dreaming of this ideal state of travel. Normally, one needs the temperament of a sage, the resolution of an army mule, and the toes of a gladiator to survive the rigors of second-class Indian transportation. But this compartment was empty, and a cool breeze swooshed in through the open windows, so I had a pleasant trip. I admired the small farms lush with different crops and flowers, the carefree children, the bored buffaloes, the thatched houses, and the magnificent temples and mosques.

I noticed that though the poor live in the most basic conditions, they still make certain that the gods are accommodated in style. It really is heartwarming. A poor man will go through life with a perpetual leaking roof but will make certain that his deities live in comfort.

I arrived in Manmad with mixed emotions. I sincerely hoped that the family still lived there. Often, when tragedy of this type thrusts itself on a family, there is a physical as well as an emotional uprooting of the family. I wondered if the Wadhwani family still lived in Manmad. If they did, were they still occupying their original dwelling?

I walked down the narrow lanes of the village and saw images of Lord Ganesha everywhere. It was the first of several days devoted to Lord Ganesha. With love and care, family members carried him to their homes, where they would pamper and fuss over him.

I made a few inquiries and was directed to the Wadhwanis' house. It was a two-story building with long corridors. Mr. Wadhwani lived with his family on the first floor in the extreme right-hand corner. I virtually collided with a group of children, who like children everywhere were trying their best to bring the building down.

"Is this where Mr. Wadhwani lives?" I asked hesitantly. The children halted and observed me with a jaundiced eye.

"Yes. Who are you?" asked one of them.

"Who are you?" I asked.

"We are his children," they said in unison.

"All of you!" My eyes opened wider.

"Except this guy with red pants. Who are you?"

"I am from Pune. I need to talk to your dad."

"Why?" asked a voice from behind me.

I turned around to answer and found myself face-to-face with a thin woman, her brow creased with anxiety and her eyes brimming with worry.

"I am from Yerwada." I found it best to stretch the truth a bit.

"I am his wife. Please come in." The look of utter confusion on my face must have prompted her to say softly, "I am his first wife. Please come in."

I entered her humble home. The children followed. Her home was clean, filled only with the necessities of life.

"What can I do for you?"

"I was in Yerwada a few weeks ago, and I met Rehana."

"How is Rehana *didi* [sister]?" She was genuinely worried about Rehana, her husband's second wife. (In some segments of Indian society, it is not uncommon to have more than one legal wife.)

"How is *chotti ma* [little mother]?" inquired the eldest of the children. He was a boy of ten or twelve years. His name was Ramu.

"She is as well as you can be while in prison. She is very worried about her daughter and why her husband has not answered the letters from her and the prison staff."

"What letters? We did not get any letters from them. Why would they write to us?"

"Rehana's son . . ."

"How is Shyam *bhaiya* [brother]?" Once again the oldest boy, Ramu, interrupted.

"He is all right, but as he is already five years old, he has been put into an orphanage. Rehana wanted him to stay with all of you. She is also worried about Mr. Wadhwani's health. Is he all right?"

"No. He is not at all well. Because of his ill health, he can barely work. There are many mouths to feed, and he is the sole earning member of our family," Mrs. Wadhwani explained. Tears gathered in her eyes. "Let me bring you something to eat."

"No, no, please."

"You must eat something. You have come from far."

"Please, I want nothing." It was obvious her feelings were hurt. "Will you make me a cup of tea?"

"I will. Please be comfortable." She left the room.

"This is *chotti ma's* daughter, my sister." The eldest boy tenderly pushed a small girl toward me. She stood with her hands on her hips. It was obvious that she was well cared for and that she was happy. Her eyes twinkled.

"Do you miss your mother and brother Shyam?"

"I like it here. I did not like it in jail. *Badi ma* [elder mother] takes care of me, and now I am going to school." Saying this, she ran off to be with her brothers and sisters.

"I don't go to any school," said Ramu. He was dressed in clean clothes, and his hair was neatly brushed. It was obvious that he spent considerable time in front of the mirror.

"Why don't you go to school?"

"Oh, I fell from the first floor and landed straight on my head and now I can't remember anything, so I don't go to school."

This boy had a good thing going for him!

"You're lying, Ramu."

"No, I am not."

"He fell on his fat head and now he is enjoying life," teased a curly-headed youngster in yellow pants.

"Don't listen to him, Uncle. He is jealous. I fell straight on my head," Ramu insisted.

"Like a football—he looked very funny!"

"One blow and your head will also be like a football. Really, Uncle, I swear. I can't remember anything. But tell *chotti ma* I miss her a lot. Tell her, okay? Don't forget like I do."

"No, I won't forget." I took the cup of tea and thanked his mother. "Where is Mr. Wadhwani?"

"He is out looking for work. He has not been well for a long time." It was obvious the woman was suffering. She had five children—four of her own and the other from her husband's second wife. I could not suggest that she take on another child. Six children, an ailing husband, and no source of income? It was apparent that they were living hand to mouth. The children gathered around her. It was apparent that they all loved her. I finished the tea and stood up to leave, when my eye fell on a small shrine to Lord Ganesha. Ma Durga was by his side. I could hear a chant welcoming Lord Ganesha. Reverently, I touched him and Ma Durga before leaving an offering.

Mrs. Wadhwani said, "Give my love to Rehana. She is like a younger sister to me. Tell her we pray for her daily and not to worry about her daughter. She is my daughter, too. As soon as her father is well, I will send him to visit her."

I nodded. I patted Ramu on the head and slowly descended the rickety stairway. There was a long journey ahead—a seven-hour bus trip to Pune. Again I wished a social organization in Nasik had made this trip years ago to give Rehana a bit of peace of mind. It was either a lack of manpower or money, or perhaps working with sorrow and misery day after day, even social workers have become habituated to the agony of the mother inmate.

A month later Mr. Wadhwani died, leaving six children and two women destitute.

A Heartrending Reunion for Poornima

One day Shenaz telephoned to tell me that Poornima's children were arriving in two days to meet with their mother. Poornima, the mother of three children, had been sentenced to life in prison and had not seen her children for two years. The reason was simple: money—or the lack of it. That this poor woman was going to see her children after two long years was good news indeed. I was not certain I wanted to be present when this reunion took place. For some reason it felt like an intrusion into their world, which was already brimming with sorrow.

But Shenaz said, "Poornima insists that you be present. She wants her children to meet the person who has made this trip possible. You have helped her. She has great hope in you. She hopes you can help get the children into a boarding school."

After hanging up, I once again felt low and disheartened. If in a jail like Yerwada, in a city like Pune, a mother went without seeing her child for two years for lack of 1,000 rupees, I wondered about the situation in remote parts of the country. The government cannot be held responsible for everything. Social workers, NGOs, and citizens with compassionate hearts must help.

Two days later, I found myself back in Madam Kadam's office. The kittens were nowhere around. I was told that they had gone for a stroll. Shenaz had yet to arrive. This was the visiting hour. At the extreme left, a *sardarji* (a man with a turban) spoke to his imprisoned wife. They were young—still in their mid-thirties. They seemed to be from respectable backgrounds. What could the woman have done to be in jail? As a child, even in her remotest nightmare, she must never have envisioned that she would end up in prison. She appeared to have an upbringing that spoke of education and love.

Then I realized that Poornima's children had at last arrived. There was a lot of wailing. Poornima's cry was heartbreaking. Off and on, she would beseech God for mercy. Then I saw a small child walk out of the dingy visiting room. He stood between the two gates of Yerwada—one that faces the world and the other that imprisons the women. He walked out of the visiting room and then vomited. Was it the raw emotion or the dingy room and suffocating heat?

Poornima's sister-in-law, who tends the children, was an old woman dressed in ethnic Maharashtrian garb. She made the child drink water and then went with him to sit outside in the open air. Seeing them go, Poornima broke into sobs once more.

Then Shenaz arrived. She told me that the three children and three adults had arrived from Nagpur. They would be here for a day or two. She was trying to organize their stay in one of the homes run by the many social organizations in Pune. The entire cost of this trip to bring Poornima's children to visit her was 1,200 rupees. A day earlier, two close friends took me to lunch. Three entrées, coffee, and a couple of hours of indigestion later, they had forked out the same amount.

I hesitated, but Shenaz suggested we go in to get a feel for the situation. Seeing us, Poornima rose from the other side of the partition.

"*Bhai* [brother], my own son does not recognize me. You saw him. He does not recognize me. My own son does not know me. And he looks so tiny. Does he look like a five-year-old boy? He looks as though he is just three years old. This is because he misses me. This is my daughter."

To her daughter, Vasudha, she said, "Touch his feet. He is my brother. It is because of him you are here."

Poornima's daughter was about thirteen years old. Her eyes were those of an old woman who has seen untold misery and humiliation. She was no longer a child. Fate and circumstances had aged her. I could imagine her mother's plight. Should she weep for her daughter's lost childhood, or should she fear for the young girl who stood on the threshold of womanhood? I could only imagine Poornima's

state of mind. Fear and agony, mixed with anger and impotency—a nightmarish concoction.

Vasudha's brother sat near her. He was about nine years
old, without a care in the world. Obviously, his sister had
borne the brunt of their mother's absence. There was another man sitting next to the children. I was told he was
a friend and a well-wisher.

"Tell me, Shenaz, does Poornima's sister-in-law gain
financially by making certain that the children stay with her
and not go to a boarding school?"

"We are giving her 200 rupees per child."

"For them 600 rupees is not a small sum."

"Exactly. Also, they want Poornima to sign a few documents. Once she does that, the children get their father's
Provident Fund and other benefits," Shenaz explained.

"That must be quite an amount."

"For them it certainly is."

"If the children are lodged in a boarding school, is the
money then kept in their name?"

"Yes, and thus Poornima's sister-in-law gets nothing."

"Does Poornima have to sit behind that dreadful partition? Can't she hold her children? Where's she going to run
to anyway?"

"I'll talk to somebody in charge."

"And get this strange man out of here so she and the
children can talk freely among themselves."

The man was asked to wait outside the jail. He went,
assuring me that he had no stake or claim in the whole
business and was just a family friend.

As soon as the children were alone with their mother,
Poornima turned to me and Shenaz.

"I don't want the children to go back. Shenaz *didi* [sis-
ter], please put them in a boarding school right now.
Brother, you know why they have come here. They want

me to sign these papers that will entitle them to all my husband's money. Then they'll treat my children like servants. They do not feed them properly and do not send them to school. Her children go to school, but my children are sent to work in the fields. They wear torn clothes while her children wear the best of clothes. Oh God, I want to die! Kill me! I cannot take this anymore!" She could not go on and began slapping her palm against her forehead.

While Shenaz and the prison guard tried to comfort Poornima, I went outside. Vasudha and her brother followed me. They were both crying.

"Do you want to go to a boarding school?" I asked Vasudha. She was just thirteen years old, but her face resembled her mother's and her eyes were filled with pain.

"I want to study, but they say that if I want to study, I must go away and leave my brothers with them. I can't leave my brothers. I have to take care of them. Yes, I want to go to a boarding school, but only if I can be with my brothers." Her reasons were clear. She would endure misery and hardship, forsaking her happiness and freedom, to make certain that her two brothers were not mistreated or deprived in her absence.

"Why didn't you write to Shenaz didi and explain this?"

"They won't allow me to write to anyone and I don't have any money. They don't want me to go to school, and when I am in the fields, I can't write. When I am at home I am working, so there's no time and I have no money." She began to cry. Her brother sat by her side and stared at us. He honestly seemed bored to death with all the drama around him. I doubted that he was upset about not having his share of education.

He said to Vasudha, "Why are you crying? I will work with you in the fields."

"Shut up! You shall study," she said to her brother.

"He's so stupid. He does not understand what is going on. They allow him to play and waste his time, so he's happy. You will study." The boy nodded. It was obvious that he held his sister in awe—as well he should!

Suddenly, the inner gate opened and Poornima ran out and hugged her children. They all began to cry and held each other for a long time. I went back to Madam Kadam's office until I heard Poornima call for me. She and the children were sitting on the floor, near the edge of the inner gate. Someone had brought them food. Poornima fed her children. Vasudha ate slowly, but tears kept rolling down her cheeks.

"Brother, may God always bless you and your family."

"Poornima, just be with your children and don't worry. Shenaz will make certain that they go to a boarding school starting next year."

From Shenaz, I learned that if Saathi desired, the three children could be placed in a government boarding school in Pune next year. They would be close to their mother and would be able to meet with her more often. Obviously, it is important to have social organizations work hand in hand with government institutions. It makes a world of difference for the deprived and the underprivileged.

After they had eaten and the guards were gone, Vasudha surreptitiously handed me a letter for Shenaz. I put a little money in her hand.

"Use the money to write to your mother or Shenaz. Keep it carefully."

The last thing I saw as the gates of Yerwada closed was two children clinging to their mother.

tihar—the largest prison
in the asia pacific

TO BE FAIR, HALF OF MUMBAI warned me about Delhi's mercurial weather. Apart from dressing up like an Eskimo, I was advised to carry a suitcase bursting with clothes suitable for a polar bear. The plane touched down at the Delhi airport in pouring rain. Delhi was dark, wet, cold, and dismal. Because of the smog and mist, I could barely see beyond the end of my nose.

I took the luggage to my room at the Parsi Sanatorium—a lovely one-story building with a serene fire temple in the complex, a garden, and a hypersensitive dog named Ralf. Located in the heart of Delhi, the rooms have basic comforts at a reasonable price. It is no wonder that the place is frequented by most Parsis. (Originally from Persia, the Parsi community has been living in India for more than seven hundred years.)

Tihar jail is a half hour from the Parsi Sanatorium. On the way there, I reviewed what I knew about it. From Dr. Kiran Bedi's book, *It's Always Possible,* I learned that Tihar was a hellhole when she took over as inspector general. She and her successor are responsible for its metamorphosis into India's model jail.

Tihar had been ruled by rampant corruption, the power of money, and brute force. It was overcrowded, and the quality of food, medical services, hygiene, sanitation, and the general quality of life were notoriously bad. Inhumane conditions prevailed. It is hard to believe that here in the capital of India that human beings, most of them yet to be convicted of a crime, were leading lives worse than those of animals.

Here is what Kiran Bedi told me in an interview about conditions in Tihar when she took the post of inspector general:

"I was now the head of the Tihar jail system, the largest prison system in the Asia Pacific. In 1993, the Tihar jail

complex housed four prisons that served as 'judicial cus-
todians' for more than 7,200 inmates. The complex had
a sanctioned capacity of 2,273." Worse, she also told me that
at that time only 10 percent of those in Tihar jail had been
convicted. The remaining 90 percent were on remand, waiting for trial in various courts. She went on:

"There were 46 children up to the age of five staying with
their mothers in prison. Some had been born in jail. There
was no child specialist, no immunization program for the
children, and no night female doctor to attend to them. At
night, prisoners looked after themselves. Even with so many
children, there was no nursery to isolate them for even a short
time during the day. Women prisoners were subjected to the
most humiliating experiences, which robbed them of what
little dignity and self-respect they had left. It is nothing short
of a miracle that these women managed to cling to their san-
ity, despite the overwhelming odds they faced."

Here is what one of the inmates revealed about the state
of affairs in Tihar in 1990:

"I came here on October 2, 1990. One of the staff, who is
gone now, used to come into the ward and paw the women.
He was also in the habit of calling some of the women prisoners to his office, even in the daytime. In the women's ward,
a sort of mafia ruled. These gangsters were extorting money
from people with big cases and who had big money. Then
they bribed the staff to manipulate the visitations so that they
could have *mulaqaats* (meeting time) every day. The food in
the prison was very bad. Chapatis (flat bread) were wrapped
in the rag that was used for mopping the floors and left lying
out in the courtyard for hours. This was a routine practice.
Magisterial inspection of the prison took place once a month.
At that time, all the prisoners were locked up. Only one or
two prisoners were brought out to speak to the magistrate.
The lawyers were on their own moneymaking trip. The free

legal-aid lawyer might as well not have been there. She was useless. The lawyer I engaged duped me after charging an enormous amount of money. He had assured me that he would get me bailed out. When I attended court, I realized to my horror that he had made an application in court to summon all my witnesses. So, instead of trying for a speedy disposal of my case, he was suggesting a fresh trial."

Another inmate spoke emotionally about the appalling conditions that existed in the prison during the early 1990s:

"In the case of delivery, if the woman happened to give birth while she was still in the barracks, there was no medical help available between 1:00 p.m. and 10:00 a.m. This was because the doctor would come to work only at 10:00 a.m. and leave at 1:00 p.m. So we assisted the woman in birth. We had nothing, not even a first-aid box, and no one to help. In one case, a woman delivered her baby, but we had nothing to cut the umbilical cord. The child was lying outside for a long time (attached to the mother). We desperately searched for anything sharp, but we found nothing. Finally, we got a small piece of blade from a woman in the same dormitory, but it was too many hours after the delivery, and the baby died.

In another case, a woman delivered at night, during the lock-in period. No medical attendant came for her. In the morning, when the barracks opened, we went inside and saw her lying with all the blood and the outflow. No one had washed the child. We bathed the baby, and one of us cleaned up the woman. The fellow inmates of her dormitory had left her on her own in a corner of the barrack."

This was the experience of a woman inmate arrested for a narcotics offense. Even the staff was not happy about the conditions that existed in Tihar. A few women officers narrated their experiences to Dr. Bedi:

"I have been in service for more than six years and have

seen the conditions in the women's ward of Tihar jail from the closest quarters possible. I felt sorry for their children, whose ages ranged from babes in arms to toddlers and four-years-olds. There were no facilities for special food for them. After considerable effort, I was able to arrange *khichadi* (a kind of rice and vegetable broth) for the little ones. There were no educational facilities for either the women or children. Many women expressed great anxiety about their children being left unattended outside while they were serving time in prison."

According to Dr. Kiran Bedi, "The prison atmosphere, with its undercurrents of violence, tension, bitterness, and distrust, had an adverse psychological impact on the children who were staying there with their mothers. The claustrophobic conditions drastically curtailed their natural instincts to frolic and romp around and indulge in playful activities."

The necessity of nurseries and a separate cell for women living with their children is highlighted by the following narrative from an official who worked with the children in Tihar:

"They were not children, they were little monsters. They would abuse you like adults and spoke the language of violent criminals, such as 'I will kill you,' 'I'll murder you,' or 'I'll shoot you,' 'I will stab her in the stomach.' Even under the age of four, they were indulging in homosexual acts and making sexual advances. On being scolded, they would become abusive and throw stones at us. They were violent with the insects and frogs they found in the jail. They would crush them, tear them, burn them, and squeeze them alive. They would pick up live frogs and throw them at us. No one could handle them."

To me, this is why it should be mandatory for all Indian prisons to have a nursery for children living with their mothers. These children should spend the day constructively and be taught with love and care. Their childhood should be as normal as possible. If not, the prison authorities are only making certain that these children are taught and influenced by the hardened criminals of the prison. Left with criminals and without any support from social organizations, these children, unfortunate shadows in cages, are deprived of any semblance of a normal life.

We were now approaching the prison. It started raining again. I cursed. The driver added a few uncomplimentary and unprintable comments about nature in general and Delhi in particular.

"You have somebody living in Tihar?" he asked.

"No. I am writing a book on Indian jails."

"Now Tihar is very good. Sometimes I wish I could live there."

I thought the cold and the chattering of my teeth had disturbed my hearing. I shifted the pullover that I had wrapped over my face and ears.

"Why would you want to live in Tihar?"

"Sahib, sometimes after working so hard, there is still too little money to support myself and the family. At least if we were in Tihar, the problem of eating and surviving would be taken care of."

Obviously things had improved at Tihar.

We pulled to a stop outside the largest jail in the South-Asia Pacific. I was about to find out exactly how much the prison had improved.

A Better Life in Tihar

I must admit that Mr. Ajay Agarwal, the director general of Tihar prisons (who recently retired), and Mr. Sunil Gupta, the highly regarded law officer of Tihar, were professional and the absolute antithesis of stereotypical government officials. It has become a custom in India to berate anything that has even the shadow of officialdom. In fact, blaming the government for everything, even a bad monsoon, seems to be one of the prerequisites of Indian citizenship.

It had taken only a few e-mails, a dozen phone calls, and a fax to get the green light to enter Tihar—no minor miracle, given that I had permission not only to enter but also to interview the inmates and then publish my findings uncensored.

After convincing the guards that I had no intention of blowing up Tihar jail's head office, I was shown to the office of Mr. Gupta. I entered, shook hands with him, and sat down. Another meeting was already in progress.

"Although what is happening in Tihar is heartening and good, don't you think Tihar is sending the wrong message to society?" Mr. Gupta looked at the elderly lady posing this question as he tried to answer two phone calls simultaneously.

"What wrong message are we sending to society, madam?"

"The conditions in Tihar, at least for women with children, are so good that for a poor woman with a small child, it is better to be inside Tihar than outside. In Tihar, you have all the facilities to take care of your child and yourself, while outside, thousands of poor women and children barely manage one meal a day."

"Madam, our job is to make certain that Tihar is a place where reformation takes place. You cannot initiate reform without rehabilitation."

"But sir, if you enter the jail, it seems as though the women have never had it so good. If you go in now, you will see women sitting out in the sun, some drying their hair, some at work earning good money, the children well fed and enjoying themselves. I am not saying anything is wrong with that, but the fact is that many of these women are murderers and have committed other heinous crimes. Some have killed their daughters-in-law. Some have murdered their husbands. Some are here for peddling drugs. It's true many of them are in prison due to circumstances such as poverty. But don't you think that while serving a penal sentence, not everyone should have access to these amazing rehabilitation programs? Let the reforms reach those who are in prison for crimes committed due to circumstances such as poverty, or where they are the real victims, rather than letting everybody, even cold-blooded murderers and hardened criminals, enjoy the benefits of rehabilitation."

"A good point, but who is to decide the moral aspect of a crime committed? A woman may have killed her husband for various reasons. How are we to decide if she has killed her husband because he was constantly abusing her or because she had fallen in love with someone else and thought that her husband was better off dead? Who is to decide who the reforms should reach? Yes, what you say is true to a large extent, but there is no solution. Who is going to decide what is grain and what is chaff?" He looked at me and again picked up the telephone, asking the caller to call back.

"Sorry about the phone calls. Where was I? Yes, you know that often when a woman is six or seven months pregnant, she gets thrown into Tihar on purpose. You know why? Because the facilities that we provide pregnant women and those who have just given birth are so excellent that the woman decides that to be in prison is best for her and her child. Thus, Tihar has borne the cost and taken care of pregnant women who enter a few months before delivery and leave when the baby is three or four months old.

We can't do anything about it. The care, the diet, the medication, the facilities all are much better than what the woman could afford on her own. So, many of them decide to let the government of India foot the bill and the NGOs provide the service and the care." He once again juggled with the phones.

"At one point there was a rumor that women under the care of the Tihar authorities delivered only boys. Since baby boys are so highly valued, you can well imagine the rush to enter Tihar. Eventually, in a tactful manner through the media and word of mouth, the Tihar authorities spread the message that there was a statistical error and 'fewer boys and more girls' seemed to prefer the accommodations at Tihar. Since then, things have rather quieted down and Tihar is no longer held in such high esteem."

When we were alone, Sunil Gupta made certain that I was given an official letter, giving me permission to enter Tihar Central Jail No. 6A, where women prisoners are lodged, the next day.

Inside Tihar Central Jail No. 6A

I woke up with a start. It was freezing cold. My breath hung in the air like smoke. Someone was knocking at my door with a persistent zeal.

"What?" I yelled. Whoever it was did not bother to reply but persisted in knocking. I put my feet on the floor and nearly hit the ceiling. The floor felt a few notches below zero degrees. I cursed aloud and, throwing a blanket around myself, went to the door.

There was nobody in sight. Something hit me hard on the knee, and then I saw him—a shaggy white dog looking up at me, a cup held tightly in his smiling mouth. Perhaps

I was a sight to be seen, wrapped in a blanket from head to toe, with only a nose showing through.

I scolded him anyway. "There are at least fifty rooms here and you chose mine to knock at. And stop staring at me." In reply, he dropped the cup hard on my toes. A man-to-man conversation on proper timing and behavior ensued. I also elaborated on the importance of reaching Tihar and concluded by emphasizing that if it did not hurt his feelings, could he please knock on somebody else's door and let me brave a bath in this appalling foul weather?

Bathed and wearing half my wardrobe, I entered the fire temple to pay obeisance to the holy fire. (For Parsis, fire is the most important form of God. In their temples a holy fire is kept burning for hundreds of years.) Then I caught a rickshaw to the outer gate of Jail No. 6A, which housed women and children. It began to rain, and a cold draft and heavy fog materialized. The security guard read the letter signed by Sunil Gupta and then grudgingly granted me access. I walked on as directed and a few minutes later came to a huge wall that turned and twisted like an enormous snake. Security guards were perched on top. One of them challenged me.

"Where in hell do you think you are going?" I waved the letter from Sunil Gupta at him and suggested he read it. He was perched fifty feet above the ground and did not find my answer amusing. From nowhere, another guard materialized. He tried to snatch the letter, but I held onto it. He could barely read it but grunted that I could move on. He shouted to his crony on the watchtower something like, "It would be best to shoot this guy, but we'll have to let him walk away—hard luck."

Fifty meters away stood the massive inner gate of Jail No. 6A. It is much like the Yerwada gate, except the latter can be seen from the main road in Pune, while this jail is hidden from public view. I pushed the letter through one of the slots and was allowed entry. The gate closed behind me, and about twenty meters ahead stood the gateway into the main complex. I was asked to relinquish all money, cigarettes, tobacco, guns, knives, and bullets, and was searched. After signing two registers, I was finally free to enter the main jail complex.

First I visited Sunita Sabharwal, superintendent of the women's wing of the Central jail. We chatted about the welfare of the children and set a time for an interview the following day after my cursory observation of the jail.

Oddly, though I had been to Yerwada jail frequently, I had never been allowed to enter the prison itself. Here in Tihar, I was inside with minimal fuss and red tape. It said a lot about the transparency with which this mammoth prison functions—authors, the media, and filmmakers have access without censorship. For this we should be thankful to past Inspector Generals Kiran Bedi and I. K. Gupta, as well as Ajay Agarwal, the director general who recently retired.

After a cup of hot tea, Sunita Sabharwal sent a security guard with me to meet Neetu Chugh, the assistant superintendent. On the way, he showed me groups of women working at different handicrafts. The women either bowed their heads in a *namaste* greeting or continued to work.

Neetu Chugh, who was seven months pregnant, gave me a tour of the jail, starting with the kitchen. Before the reforms were initiated, the hygiene conditions of the kitchen were notoriously bad. I observed that the present kitchen was extremely clean. To enter it, I had to remove my shoes and wear special slippers provided by the staff. Three women were preparing rice in massive metallic urns. Neetu asked if I could taste the food, but lunch was over and now they were just starting dinner. The meals—rice, dal, vegetables, and chapatis—were freshly prepared. As we stepped into the main compound that housed the different cells and vocational centers, it began to rain again—not rain, pour. Umbrellas materialized, and we began the tour.

There were eight wards, and, believe me, they looked more like those built in ashrams and health-care centers. On that day, there were 506 inmates and 41 children. Well-trimmed green grass surrounded the complexes that house the inmates. From where I stood, it was hard to believe that I was in a prison. Most residents of Mumbai don't live in such an ambience. In fact, there is a water-harvesting program in all the jails in the Tihar complex, and around seven thousand saplings have been planted to make the environment eco-friendly. Previously, Tihar had been a cement jungle. It goes to show what a few individuals with initiative can do and what a few simple changes can do to improve the lives of countless people.

This is not to say that prison is not a cage. However fancy it is from the outside, the reality is that you have no privacy and no freedom and are at the mercy of the authorities. If they take a dislike to you, then God help you. Another problem in most jails, including Tihar, is the abominable overcrowding.

I was shown the place allotted for handicraft work. Neetu informed me that the inmates spend the day at handicrafts, and, ironically, eventually earn enough to support their families living outside the prison. Income-generating programs for female prisoners include weaving, stitching, and cooking. Another important and heartening point to note is that education is required for all female prisoners. In fact, special attention is given to illiterate inmates so that within a week's time the prisoner is able to write his or her name. I was told that 1,861 women inmates were given vocational training in 2002, and there were provisions for both formal and non-formal education.

"There are times when these inmates have 10,000 or

15,000 rupees saved in the bank, all due to the support of and work brought in by different NGOs, namely India Vision Foundation (IVF). They send money to their families," Neetu explained.

Neetu then took me to the nursery begun by India Vision Foundation under the leadership of Dr. Kiran Bedi. There are two nursery facilities for the children and a special diet for children and expectant mothers. It is also heartening to note that in Tihar there are regular visits by pediatricians and gynecologists.

The moment the children saw us, they folded their pudgy little hands into the *namaste* greeting. There were at least twenty children, ranging from a few months old to four or five years. The infants were in a cradle, cared for by two inmates assigned to this job. A social worker from the India Vision Foundation was teaching the children to read and write the English alphabet. It was obvious from the children's happy, healthy faces what a world of difference a well-run nursery makes to the lives of so many innocent children. They wore clean uniforms specially stitched by IVF. Most important of all, they looked happy. They study, play, and nap on clean mats, eat a nourishing meal, and then in the evening go back to their mothers.

"With the children here, the mother has time to work and earn money. Also, here in the nursery the children play only with other children and are treated like children, thus retaining their childhood. Away from their cells and that adult environment, they can study and play and just be children. IVF staff take them for picnics and other excursions on a regular basis," Neetu explained. In contrast, in other jails in the country the children rarely see the outside world.

I nodded in understanding. It didn't matter how many reforms were initiated. If children didn't spend time away from the politics and emotional baggage of their elders, they would never really be free to experience the joy of childhood. They could forget, for a while at least, that they were in prison. Obviously, it is essential to have a special space in every prison allotted to the children. Why should they suffer for the fault of their mothers? They are shadows of their mothers, and it is already heartwrenching that these shadows have been caged; at least their misery should not spill over to every waking hour.

Neetu led me to another ward. The women's wing in Tihar has one area dedicated to mothers and their children. There is another area for those women who have recently entered Tihar. It is essentially a place to give them a few months to acclimatize to the prison system. After admission, a prisoner is counseled by welfare officers and other staff members. This is another service not available in most prisons in India. I wonder why.

Neetu now led me to a huge cottagelike structure dedicated to acclimatization. In a large open space with dormitories and cells, a number of inmates sat in the open space just outside their cells. Some were eating, while others sat combing their hair or just hanging around. They all wore thick cardigans or had shawls wrapped around themselves. The sight of so many women and children spending their lives in a fancy cage disheartened me and numbed my senses.

I stood at the door of one of the quarters. It was a cylindrically shaped room. Bulbs threw in bright golden light. Individual bedrolls were spread out on the floor, and it was obvious that overcrowding had virtually annulled most of the phenomenal reforms that had been initiated in Tihar. But with millions of people living hand to mouth and without a roof over their heads, it is unfair to expect prisons to have all the comforts. The TV was on, a few women were sewing, and two were sweeping the area in which they slept and kept their meager belongings. On the extreme left was the open toilet surrounded by a small wall about three or four feet high.

Unlike Yerwada, here in Tihar there are fans, which must be a blessing to combat Delhi's scalding heat. Today, obviously, nobody needed fans; it was freezing cold. I looked at the inmates one last time, all safely tucked in their blankets. I was told that each inmate is given a few blankets to use as a bedroll, and also a few blankets to cover themselves. I looked at them almost enviously—here I was, partially wet and shivering, trying my best to keep my teeth from tap-dancing on each other.

"May I see where the children live?"

Neetu explained, "The children and their mothers live together in a separate ward. Unlike other jails, where children are kept in the same cell as every other inmate—and you know there are various types of criminals within the prison—here in Tihar we have made certain that the children and their mothers live separately from the others."

The area that lodged the mothers and children was similar to the assimilation area. The beds were rolled on the floor. There were a few women lying on their beds. I noticed a few of the children with their mothers. Neetu explained that when a child was ill or did not want to leave his or her mother (for whatever reason), the child skipped the nursery time. The windows were partially shut, and although it was warm, it was also stuffy and claustrophobic. I do not wish to downplay the initiatives and reforms going on. But overcrowding is something that jail authorities can do little about. That is something only the judicial system in our country can address.

Overcrowding is rampant in virtually every jail in the country. At present, the total lodging capacity of all six central prisons in the Tihar jail complex is around 3,637

prisoners. The last published survey shows that in the year 2002, there were 12,041 prisoners lodged there. This is more than three times the capacity of the prison. Worse, only 2,333 were convicted. Another 9,656 were waiting for trial and 52 were detainees.

The capacity of the women's prison is around 400 prisoners. At the time of my visit, it housed 506 adults and 41 children. Compared with the other jails, such as the Arthur Road jail in Mumbai, which has four times its sanctioned capacity, the Central jail for women prisoners in Tihar is far better off. Keep in mind the official capacity is itself packed bumper to bumper.

In the women's prison a store carries essentials such as soap, oil, and biscuits that can be purchased with coupons. No money is allowed within the jail, and whatever is earned is either put aside in the inmate's account or converted into coupons. With these coupons, the women can buy what they need for themselves and their children.

Since Dr. Kiran Bedi's tenure, cigarettes and tobacco are banned. Earlier, the use of drugs, cigarettes, and tobacco was rampant. With the ban, problems related to addiction have also been taken care of. In fact, Tihar jail's rehabilitation program has been widely acclaimed and adopted by other countries. I'm told that nearly 7,817 prisoners underwent treatment in 2002.

We passed by the pharmacy, and Neetu informed me that apart from regular visits made by pediatricians and gynecologists, there is around-the-clock medical care provided by female medical/paramedical staff. Not many jails in India have this essential service. Until Dr. Bedi was appointed inspector general of Tihar jail in 1993, inmates of Tihar suffered inhumane treatment as far as health care was concerned. As mentioned earlier, there was no medical help at all during the night, and even during the day it took the grace of God to get help.

What a contrast to the current situation! It just goes to show that when the management adopts a humanitarian approach and the NGOs cooperate, miracles can happen. Reformation and positive transformation take place with right and noble intentions, not through mere enforcement of the law.

After my tour of Tihar, I left the women's prison and decided to visit Sunil Gupta again. For some reason, I decided not to use the conventional main road, and instead I took the inner road that connected Jail No. 6A to the head office. After half an hour of intense walking through wet mud, dodging puddles, construction debris, and heavy gusts of wind, I arrived at exactly the same spot that I had started from—back at Jail No. 6A. I guess even if a prisoner escaped and wanted to avoid the main road, it would take an intricate map and all the blessings from the protective Masters to get out of this maze! Eventually, a passing security guard pointed me in the right direction.

By then I was exhausted. I stopped and lit a cigarette. I must have been out of my mind. Everywhere "No Smoking" signs loomed large and clear. I philosophized that at worst I would find myself behind bars, and then at least I would have dry clothes and food.

Then I saw a man in his shorts riding a bicycle and carrying a machine gun in one hand. My first thought was how could any sane man ride a bicycle in shorts in this frightful weather? My second thought was why was this crazed man carrying a machine gun? Do they shoot people who smoke in Tihar? In that case, smoking really would be not only dangerous for your health but also fatal. He passed me by and I threw out the cigarette that I had somehow managed to hide in my mouth.

Do Prisoners Have Rights?

The tolling of the fire temple bells woke me the next morning. The familiar clang of the bells heartened my weary body, reminding me of my childhood and the home where my cousins and I lived with our grandmother. Every few hours, the air resounded with the tolling of these bells and was filled with the fragrance of sandalwood. I must have heard it a thousand times, sleeping on my double-decker bed. Now, a thousand miles away, I ached for my childhood. I thought of the children in prisons and orphanages waking up each day without the warmth, comfort, and security of loved ones and a place to call home.

Nearly an hour later, I was seated once again in the office of Sunil Gupta. I had many questions about prison procedures.

"Why do different prisons have different rules for prisoner welfare? Tihar has a published jail manual but it is applicable only for the inmates of Tihar. Why is there no uniformity in jail manuals?"

Mr. Gupta explained, "There is only one penal code and it is uniformly applicable in all the states in India, but there are special acts under which prisoners are tried, sent to jail, and prosecuted. According to the constitution of India, the state can pass its own legislature pertaining to the governing of jails in that state. Thus, each state has its own jail manual. Most states have copied the *Punjab Jail Manual,* and they have formulated their manual to suit their convenience."

"Unlike Tihar's jail manual, which has been drafted keeping the inmates in mind?"

"Exactly."

"How old is the *Punjab Jail Manual?*"

"It is around one hundred and fifteen years old."

"You mean most jails are being run in accordance with a manual that is one hundred and fifteen years old? Obviously, the manuals are far behind the times," I answered in astonishment.

"Yes, yes."

"Is anyone updating these manuals?"

"Yes. In Delhi, a committee has prepared a *Model Prison Manual,* and we are formulating the *Delhi Jail Manual. The Delhi Jail Manual* has been applicable since February 2002."

"Tihar also has a *Prisoner's Handbook,* which is all encompassing with respect to prisoners' welfare. Is a handbook required for all prisons?" I asked.

"According to a Supreme Court ruling, each state must have its own handbook, which helps the prisoners understand their rights and duties. Unfortunately, most of the states are unaware of this ruling and only a few have complied with it."

"There are still many states that do not follow the law of the land? A mandatory ruling to publish and make available a prisoner's handbook informing every prisoner of his or her rights and duties is being ignored by many states?" I was incredulous.

"Yes, it is mandatory. Supreme Court judgments are binding on all the states."

"Now let us consider those waiting for trial. There are instances where an inmate who has committed a crime but is yet to be convicted has already spent far more time in jail than what his punishment warrants. How do the authorities at Tihar handle such a situation?"

"Here in Delhi (at Tihar), we have a tribunal that reviews each case and makes certain that someone awaiting trial, guilty or not guilty, is not kept in prison longer than his sentence would be."

"Once again, Delhi is an exception."

"Yes, that is unfortunately true. In Delhi, we are trying to follow the law, not only because it is mandatory but also because we are really trying to keep the prisoners' welfare in mind."

"What can someone waiting for trial do to make certain that the state and jail authorities obey the law?"

"Someone waiting for trial has the right to approach the High Court or even the Supreme Court. Getting justice is the fundamental right of a prisoner under Article 25 of the constitution. Thus, the prisoner can get this right enforced through the High Court or the Supreme Court," Mr. Gupta explained.

"For that, the prisoner needs a capable lawyer?"

"He can use a lawyer, or he can simply move a petition from the jail."

"Does he have to submit this through the welfare officer of the prison?"

"He can submit the petition through a relative, a friend, or through the prison authorities. It does not really matter."

"Can it simply be a handwritten letter demanding that she be granted her fundamental right?"

"Yes. The letter has to be submitted to the High Court or the Supreme Court. They have concurrent jurisdiction to enforce the fundamental rights of the prisoner guaranteed by the constitution of India."

"How practical is this suggestion? I mean, do the courts really take action on a letter from a prisoner?" I asked.

"I know of many incidents where the court has acted on a letter sent to the chief justice by a prisoner lodged in Tihar jail."

"Tihar is a role model. I doubt this system works all over the country. Anyway, tell me if a person has been imprisoned for committing a murder, and the person has already spent six years waiting for trial and then gets a life sentence, what is applicable for this person? Life imprisonment is usually fourteen years in practice."

"Those six years would be counted in the total sentence. Then, after a few years, his case would come up again for consideration for early release. For life sentences, each state has a board that reviews the case. So after fourteen years, the board may recommend early release, and then the case is sent to the governor. In 70 to 80 percent of cases, the governor grants early release," Mr. Gupta explained.

"I have seen various cases where the mother in prison has not seen her child for more than a year, and the child is in the care of a government-run orphanage. Is there a law that makes it compulsory for government facilities to arrange meetings between the child and the parent?"

"In accordance with the *Delhi Jail Manual,* a woman is allowed to keep her child up to five years of age. After that, we have a number of NGOs assisting us, like Dr. Bedi's India Vision Foundation, and they make certain the child spends about three hours with his mother once a month. If a child is admitted to a government home, the caretaker arranges a meeting once every fifteen days."

I wondered about a mother in Yerwada jail who had not visited with her two children, aged eleven and thirteen, for three years. Both children were housed in a government-run orphanage. Letters from the mother, the jail authority, and the local NGO had gone unanswered.

Mr. Gupta went on. "To see her child is a fundamental right of the mother, so if there are practical difficulties, these should be worked out at the level of the jail superintendent and the person in charge of the government home."

"What if the government home ignores the jail authorities? Madam Kadam wrote personally to the orphanage without any result."

"Then the mother has the right to petition the concerned court or the High Court to enforce her right."

"Is there a law that makes it mandatory for the government orphanage to bring the child to meet his parent at least once every few months?"

"I doubt it and if there is any provision, I am unaware of it. At least in the jail manual there is no frequency prescribed."

"Isn't it sad that there is no uniform jail manual that provides a broad uniform ruling for all the jails in the country?"

"Yes, but the good thing is that there is an *All-India Model Prison Manual* that has been prepared by a committee, of which I am a member. This is a model prison manual for the entire country. We want prisons to become more remedial and welfare oriented. This manual will be uniformly applicable to all jails in the country and, hopefully, by the end of this year, it will be passed as a law. This new prison manual will replace the one-hundred-year-old model jail manual now being used by most prisons. At this time, the manual provisions are not mandatory, but we are trying to invoke the provision of the constitution to make it mandatory for all states. In some states, there are no reforms going on in the jails, because there's no money even to pay the staff. Thus, they cannot even think about reformation. The prison is considered to be a burden to the state, and so there is no effort to improve conditions."

"But if resources are the main problem, then even if the manual is made mandatory, what difference is it going to make? The state will put its hands up, claiming that the reforms cannot be initiated as the state has no money."

"True, but once the prison manual is mandatory, then the state government can ask the central government for money to meet the provisions of the manual."

"If the provisions are not mandatory, the states have no

right to ask for funding; and then these reforms will remain on paper, just like so many other proposed reforms."

"Unfortunately true," Mr. Gupta said sadly.

"India is the only country that allows a mother to keep a young child in prison with her. Is this a good thing—to keep a child in his most formative years in a prison along with hardened criminals?"

"Yes. A child should spend his formative years with his mother. This question has been raised in the Supreme Court and most of the states favored the idea, agreeing that the mother's care is more important."

"Tihar has opened its doors to the social organizations and NGO participation. Are other jails in India as open?"

"A number of jails have begun to allow NGO participation. It is important to have NGOs participate in the ongoing reforms initiated in the prisons. In fact, in the *Model Prison Manual,* there is an entire chapter regarding the activities of NGOs in the jails."

"I suspect reforms are possible only if the person heading the prison has the welfare of the prisoners at heart."

"Absolutely true. There are enough provisions made by the constitution and by the law to elevate the life of the inmate. The main reason for non-implementation is that in most of the states, the head of the jail is from outside the prison department. Take Tihar, for example. We have an excellent head of the department. Automatically, we are the front-runners in everything. The moment the head of the department is not completely involved with reforms, then automatically things will start moving downward. In most states, the person heading the show is from another branch of the government and considers being posted to run a prison as punishment."

"What do you see as the most pressing need for jail personnel?" I asked.

"We need three types of officers to implement the corrective philosophy. One is a good psychiatrist. Another is a sensitive counselor. The third is an efficient welfare officer. Each prison needs these three essential types of officers. The welfare officer's first and foremost duty is to make the prisoner aware of his or her rights and duties, and the rules and regulations of the prison. The welfare officer is also a guide and mentor to help the inmate deal with the emotional and mental trauma of being in prison."

"I'm sure you know that in most prisons there is no welfare officer, and even if there is, he or she doesn't have a corrective or rehabilitative approach."

"Yes. Unfortunately, I am aware of this shortcoming. That is something the person heading the prison should look into and rectify. It is the job of the welfare officer to make sure prisoners are given their rights."

"So if a prison has a decent welfare officer, the quality of life of the inmates improves and there is little or no abuse?"

"Exactly. And the same with the psychiatrist. I believe that the welfare of the prisoner is going to become more and more important," Mr. Gupta continued. "Recently, the chief justice of India visited Tihar and announced changes that will reduce overcrowding in Indian prisons. Petty offenses are settled right away in the jail court *(adalat)*. If convicted, the maximum sentence is seven years. If the jail adalat can handle all those cases punishable by law up to seven years, overcrowding in prisons could become a thing of the past."

"Is the system of jail adalat mandatory? Do jails all over the country have to conduct these trials?"

"Yes, it is mandatory. In Delhi, these jail trials are held regularly. It might be that in other states, they are not. Once again we come to individual responsibility and initiative. If the person in charge of the prison wants a better life for the inmates, insists that justice prevails, and upholds the fundamental rights of the inmates, only then will positive change be possible."

"Although prisoners have rights and certain powers, most of them are not aware of their own rights," I said.

"Yes, and that is why it is so important that they be briefed about their rights and duties by the welfare officer of the jail. Also, unfortunately, sometimes they are afraid of the jail staff and thus, though they are aware of their power and rights, they refrain from asserting them."

"That is why it is so imperative to have a sensitive and dedicated welfare officer. The role of NGOs is also of paramount importance."

"NGO support can make all the difference to the welfare of the inmates," Mr. Gupta agreed.

"But the decision to allow the NGO to enter the prison and work for the welfare of the inmates is in the hands of the head of the prison. It is not compulsory to have NGOs entering and working with the prisoners."

"You're right," Mr. Gupta said. "Unfortunately, it's not mandatory. It's left to the whim and inclination of the person in charge, and that is dangerous. If the person wants to hide something or allow inhumane standards of life to prevail, nobody can force him to do otherwise. This is a big problem."

With that, my interview with Sunil Gupta ended.

Missing Mommy

India Vision Foundation places children of prisoners in residence schools. They arranged for me to visit the sisters of Assisi Convent, which runs one such school in Delhi. The Assisi Convent School is a large complex that includes a residential school for children of prisoners in a one-story gray building specially constructed for this program. This building houses around twenty children, all girls, up to the age of fifteen or until they complete their education.

Maya, a social worker who volunteers at the school, and I were taken to meet the children. They were eagerly awaiting us, and, seeing Maya, a number of the girls happily gravitated toward her. One young girl held my hand and with a broad smile made me sit down on a chair. She was the same age as my daughter.

"What's your name?" I inquired in Hindi.

"Preeti. What is your name?" She asked in perfect English. I was surprised by her excellent diction.

"What is that in your hand?" Another girl inquired, again in perfect English.

"It is a tape recorder. I can record your voice, and then if you want, I can let your mother hear it. Do you want your mother to hear you?"

She nodded vigorously and her eyes got misty.

"You want to talk to your mother? Okay, here we go." I switched on the tape recorder. She held it in her hands. But her eyes brimmed with tears, and I could see her choking. She opened her mouth to speak and then shut it.

"Don't you want to speak to your mother?"

"I want to." Another girl grabbed the tape recorder from Preeti.

"What's your name?"

"Rehana."

But she also could not give a message for her mother. It was obvious that the girls wanted to talk to their mothers, but a tape recorder is a poor replacement for a mother's loving presence and gentle touch. I have realized that for these children, physical contact is very important. They constantly tried to touch us and make some kind of body contact. They held onto our fingers or our shoulders and pressed into us, subconsciously seeking the warmth and caresses that they needed so much from their parents and loved ones.

"I will speak. What shall I say? Should I talk about my exams?" Another little girl spoke in Hindi.

"Okay, that's great. Let's hear about your exams."

"But what do I say?"

"When are your exams?"

"Tomorrow."

"What grade are you in?"

"Fourth grade."

"Do you like this school?"

"Yes."

"How are the teachers?"

"They are good."

"How is the food here?"

"Good."

"Do you visit your mother every month or once every two months?" I needed to ask this question. Although everyone claimed that the children visited their mothers every month, something told me otherwise.

"Once every two months," the girl told me.

"You must be missing her the most at night?"

"Yes. I dream about her."

"So do I. I miss my papa also," said another child.

Then all the girls around me spoke about their mothers and how each child's mother visited her while she slept. Even in sleep, the body and heart longed for the mother.

"Once my mother came to visit."

"How? Where is your mother? She's not in Tihar jail anymore?"

"No, she is outside. Once in a while she phones me up."

I turned to Mr. Salegram, a school official, and asked, "Where is her mother?"

"She was released, but since she cannot take care of her child, we take care of her. She comes to visit her once in a while. We give her time with her daughter now and then, as too much interaction can cause more grief to the child. So we allow her to see the child once a month or once in two months."

Another girl came forward and stared at me and the tape recorder.

"Hi. What's your name?" I realized that not all the girls were proficient in English. So I began the conversation in Hindi and then let the girls decide which language to use.

"My name is Neha. What is that instrument?" she inquired in faultless English.

"That's a tape recorder. Were you in jail for many years?" Neha nodded.

"Five years." She kept silent then. I could only guess that she was born in Tihar.

"How old are you now?"

"I am twelve years old."

"Where is your mother?"

"Now she is out." I realized that she was not comfortable talking about her mother.

"My name is Sabrina. I was also in jail."

"For how long?"

"This I do not know." She spoke in Hindi.

"Do you remember anything about the jail?"

"Yes. I remember everything. Then it was the old jail."

"Was Kiran Bedi there?"

"Yes, she was. I know Kiran Bedi. She also knows me."

"Was the old jail good?"

She looked at Mr. Salegram.

"Tell Uncle whatever you want to tell him. Nobody is going to scold you."

"We cooked our food in our cells in the old jail. But we

were not allowed to have stoves, and if we were caught, they scolded us."

"You didn't get good food in those days in the prison?"

"In those days the food was not good."

"Now is it good?"

"Yes."

"Did you like it in Tihar?"

"No, I never liked it when somebody got hit. If they did not listen, women were hit."

"You mean women would hit other women?"

"Yes."

"Was there a lot of fighting?"

"Yes. Once there was a fight in the jail, lots of blood, and somebody's mommy was hit with a stick."

"I am also missing my mommy a lot." Another girl spoke up.

"When was the last time you saw her?"

"More than a month ago, there was a program and I met with her for a few hours. I am missing her."

"She must have been very happy to see you."

"Yes, but she cried and hugged me."

There was so much longing in her eyes that I found it difficult to breathe. I looked around and saw a sea of tears welling up in the eyes of most of the girls. Maya was surrounded by seven or eight girls, touching her hair, caressing her hand, and holding onto her. The conversation went on.

"Where is your daddy?"

"I do not have a daddy."

"What will you be when you grow up?"

"A doctor."

"I will be a teacher."

"I will be a doctor also."

"When you go to the prison to see your mother, do

you take anything with you to give to her?"

"I take a letter for her. She likes it if I write to her, so she can keep my letters and read them every day."

"My name is Nagma and my mother is in jail." One of the youngest girls spoke, tightly holding my hand.

"Your mommy is in jail?"

"Yes."

"You must be missing her."

"Yes, especially in the night."

"Did you sleep in the jail with your mommy?"

"Yes, she used to hold me tight. Now I sleep alone."

"She told me that she comes in your dreams every night and holds you tight." For a second, Nagma looked me in the eye. I held her gaze. If a man cannot lie at such times, I have no regard for honesty.

"Really?"

"Yes. Every night when you are sleeping, she holds you tight."

For a while there was silence. Then another girl came and held my hand.

"I want to talk to my mommy." I switched on the tape recorder. Then, as with the others, she had nothing to say to her. There must be so much to convey that her little heart did not know where to start. So she just stared at the machine, at her friends, and then at me.

"Come on, baby, there must be something you want to tell your mommy. Were you born in the jail?"

"Yes."

"You must have made many friends there."

"Yes. Some are here with me and some are somewhere else."

"When you visit your mother, what does she tell you?"

"She keeps telling me to study hard. Then she cries."

"She wants you to become a big person?"

"Yes. I want to become a doctor."

"You, too, want to become a doctor?"

"Yes."

"I want to be a teacher." I turned to another girl.

"What's your name?"

"Pinky."

"Where is your mommy?"

"She is in jail."

"Were you born there?"

"No. I was born at home. My mommy went to jail after I was born."

"So you have never been in jail?"

"No."

"Who brought you here?"

"Mr. Salegram."

I turned to Mr. Salegram. He was engrossed with four children who were speaking to him all at one time. He turned to me and smiled.

"When did Pinky come here?" I asked.

"1997."

"She will be here until her mother is released?"

"In all probability, Pinky will stay here until she is in tenth grade. Then we will see where she can go after that."

"Tell me your schedule. What do you do every day?" The routine was narrated by a number of children, all at the same time, and it went something like this:

"We get up at 7:30 a.m."

"That is only on a holiday."

"We get up at 5:00."

"At 5:00!" My jaw dropped.

"Yes, 5:00 on school days."

"Then we brush our teeth, bathe, get dressed, go for prayers, and come down for breakfast."

"What do you eat for breakfast?"

"On different days we get different things to eat. Then after we eat, we go to school."

"What time does school start?"

"At 7:00."

"No, it starts at 7:30."

"No, it starts at 8:00."

"You have a full day at school?"

"Yes, except on Sundays."

"Now tell me what time does school get over?"

"At 1:30 p.m."

"And then what do you do?"

"We then change our clothes."

"When do you have a bath?"

"We are coming to that. So we change our clothes, and then go for lunch, and then we wash our clothes, and then play for some time, and then we drink milk, and then we take our bath."

"You all have a bath in the afternoon?"

"Yes. And then we do our studies for the next day."

"Who teaches you?"

"Sister Gonsalves. Sister Diana teaches us math."

"Which Sister do you all like the most?" I asked.

"Sister Gladys. She has gone to Kerala. Her father died. She will come back this week."

"Okay, back to the routine. After studies, what do you do?"

"After studies, we say our prayers and then eat our food."

"What time do you eat your dinner?"

"Around 8:00 p.m. Then we watch TV."

"But not during the exams. Now we are not allowed to watch TV, but after the exams are over, we can watch TV after dinner."

"Then you all go to sleep."

"No. First we say our prayers, then we brush our teeth,

and then we go to our beds and go to sleep."

"What time do you sleep?"

"Around 9:00."

"And on Saturdays and Sundays what time do you wake up?"

"On holidays we get up at 7:30 and . . ."

"Play?"

"No. We cannot play all day. We wash up, pray, and then have breakfast. Then from 9:00 to 10:30 we study. Then at 10:30 we eat and then we play. Then we watch TV from 11:00 to 12:30. At 1:30 we eat lunch. We play until 4:00. Then comes tea and then we bathe. Then, from 7:00 to 8:00, we study. Then we pray, have dinner, watch TV, and go to sleep."

"I want to tell my mother something." Another girl held the tape recorder. I nodded. Once again there was silence.

"She wants to go back to the jail," another girl volunteered.

"Why?" I inquired.

"I like it there."

"You prefer jail to this place?"

"Yes."

"That is because, Uncle, she does not like to study. In the jail nobody forces you to study, but here you have to study. That is why she likes it in jail."

"You want to go to the jail because of that?"

"I miss my mother."

"She is lying, Uncle. She just does not like to study."

"I miss my mommy." She smiled and left with her friend. I felt a tap on my shoulder. Pinky smiled and handed me a card. It was a New Year's greeting card from her mother.

"Will you read it to me? My Hindi is very bad." She smiled at me and her eyes twinkled.

"My dear Pinky," I read, "to you I wish a Happy New Year. I hope this New Year is filled with so much happiness and that we all go to our home together as soon as possible. Dear Pinky, from your father, also, please accept a New Year's greeting. My dear child, Pinky, this year put all your heart and mind into your studies. And may you always listen to your elders and always have their blessings showering on you. January 1 is your birthday. From here, I can give you only blessings and nothing more. I pray that all the blessings that are in store for me reach you. It is morning as I write this letter. I have God's name on my lips. Child of mine, when I think of you, tears form in my eyes. My love and blessing to you, my child. From Pinky's mother to all the sisters, a Happy New Year. Also I wish a Happy New Year to Pinky's friends. I love you, Pinky."

By the time I had finished reading the card, there were tears in Pinky's eyes. For a long time I looked at the card and then at her. She composed herself and, with a smile, took the card and left the room. For a while I stood alone and observed the children. Some were bouncing around, while some stood shyly around Maya. What must it feel like to live a life with so much heartache and longing? I wondered what Pinky's mother was doing in Tihar at that very moment. It was apparent that although the children were well looked after, they longed for the human touch and the bonds that only family can provide.

reformation of a dungeon

IN APRIL, I SET OUT with Dr. Kiran Bedi's India Vision Foundation team to visit Haryana, a state adjacent to Delhi. A new prison had just opened a few months earlier in Gurgaon, Haryana. The India Vision Foundation intended to start a nursery school for the children, as well as various self-employment opportunities for the women prisoners.

The gate opened, we were admitted, and I heard the huge lock shut behind us. To the left ran a long corridor with various administrative offices. To the right were the offices of the deputy superintendent, the law officer, and a room to document and fingerprint new inmates. After a cursory search, the inner gate was unlocked and we entered the main prison campus.

Summer had just begun, and the heat was still bearable. In the glare of the sun, I saw a barren stretch of land enclosed by the ubiquitous walls that are part of the scenery in every prison and which housed various barracks. The farthest barrack was nearly a kilometer away, but fortunately for me, the women's wing was close to the main gate. In fact, it was only a two-minute walk from where we stood. We turned right and entered the gate to the women's ward.

The women's wing of Gurgaon prison has three barracks, of which only one was occupied. I was told that each barrack could house 80 inmates comfortably, but already on that day there were 125 women and 20 children in one barrack. Within a year, there would be around 200 inmates housed in each barrack. Overcrowding is common in every Indian prison, and it has become a fact of life. In fact, most prisons house at least twice (if not three times) the ward capacity. With important issues such as sanitation, abuse, malnutrition, and health at stake, quarrelling over space is looked upon as trivial.

Inside the barrack there are dormitories on each side of a fifty-foot-wide space. Thus each barrack has two dormi-

tories, and each dormitory has two sections used as rest-
rooms. All together, there are eighteen toilets and around
ten bathrooms. Though there are doors for the bathrooms,
they are open on the top and bottom. This is to prevent suicide (according to the constable), and to prevent either con-
sented or forced sex (according to an inmate). Since the
barrack is grossly overcrowded, around 100 or more inmates
share the bathrooms designed for 40. Thus, the level of hygiene reached depths that I cannot even begin to describe.

Expecting a Miracle

"Who do you want to meet?" asked one of the two female constables accompanying us. Both were young girls
but appeared perfectly capable of taking on armed robbers
in a dark alley.

"Anybody who is willing to speak with us."

"This woman speaks English and would like to talk
to you."

"Sounds good. Why is she in prison?"

"She and her lover have been accused of killing her
husband. It's a complicated case and has received lots of
publicity," explained Shakira, who is the head of the
Gurgaon project for India Vision Foundation.

Shakira and I went alone to the dormitory. Many
women inmates were sitting outside the dormitory in the
corridor, using assorted items to fan themselves. Inside the
dormitory, there were no fans. Hundreds of flies sat everywhere. Though well-ventilated and clean, the air was heavy
with an odor that characterizes prisons across the country.

Two rows of concrete slabs ran through the dormitory.
These rows are used as beds. At the base of each bed is
a cavity that is to be used for personal belongings. It appears

to be a practical arrangement, but with the excessive over-crowding, nobody knows where one so-called bed space starts or finishes. The bath and toilet area, mercifully, are separated from the sleeping quarters by a wall.

"There she is. Talk to her."

"Why don't we talk outside. It'll be less stuffy and we'll have some privacy."

The woman in question walked toward us. She looked like a college girl and was dressed in a *kurta pajama*. She seemed well educated and from a typical, humble, middle-class upbringing, ingrained with intricate moral values. Her movements were carefree, but her eyes gave her away. They spoke of confusion and agitation. Let's call her Vandana. Chairs were brought out for us, and we sat away from the glare of the sun. For a while, we observed the other prisoners, who went about their daily chores.

"Where were you before coming to this new prison?"

"In the old Gurgaon prison." Her diction and English were flawless.

"How were the conditions there?"

"Horrible." She said this looking straight ahead.

"Why was that jail horrible?"

"It was small, overcrowded, and we could not step outside."

"What do you mean by not stepping outside?" I saw her wondering whether to speak at length, or just be brief.

"Like how we are sitting now. Here we can walk around outside the dormitory and inside the barracks. But at the old jail, there was no place to walk in the open. We were in the cell for twenty-four hours. There was no going out. It was too small. Horrible. The poor children used to cry, wanting to go out and play, but there was no space, just a little veranda, which was so small that whether it was there or not made no difference. It was hell." Saying this she shook her head, as though the very thought brought back shivers of fright.

Three months later, sitting in the office of one of the top officials of Gurgaon prison, I casually inquired about the conditions of the old prison. The official looked at me and nodded in sadness.

"Don't call it a prison. It was a dungeon. It was so bad that you and I would not last in it for a day. I mean not a day. And the women's ward was not a ward; it was a small room with a capacity of four. Guess how many women were in that room?"

"Ten," I suggested hesitatingly.

"Fifty!"

"No!"

"Yes, my friend. In that old prison, in a room with a capacity for four women, there were fifty women along with children. In the end, the honorable judge from the Punjab High Court, on one of his visits, saw their plight and ordered immediate modifications to the old prison."

"Were they implemented?"

"Yes. Instead of fifty, thirty were shoved in. That was not a prison. It was a dungeon. This new prison is heaven compared with most of the prisons in the country."

I spoke again to Vandana. "How long have you been in prison?"

"Fourteen months."

"Waiting for trial?"

"Yes. I will be out soon."

"Married?"

"Yes."

One of the things I have noticed about inmates is that they either answer you without one extra word, or they ramble on, desperate to be heard.

"Your husband?"

"He is in jail, too."

"Any children?"

"One."

"Where is your child?"

"With my parents." Then once again there was a shift in her eyes, as though she needed to speak. "She is about three. She misses me a lot. But I could not let her stay with me in that old jail. It was very bad and no place for a child. Over here there are no fans. The food is not good. There is no place for a child to play or study. I can't keep her with me. But I will be leaving this place in a few days for sure, so there is no problem."

This was another sad misconception or illusion that I encountered time and again in prison. Most of the inmates were under the impression that they would be bailed out in a short while. Either bailed out or expecting that, by some miracle, the judge would realize that a major blunder had been committed and release them. Or, the government of India, along with the judiciary, would pass a new law that would either revoke or reduce their sentence. Hope is the drug that sustains them through the long, hot days and the bug-infested, claustrophobic nights.

"How is it here?" I inquired.

"It is much better than the old prison! I keep to myself. I cook my own food, I do my reading, I just keep to myself." She stood up, gave a smile that did not reach her eyes, and walked away. She looked like any typical young woman in the cities of India—educated, intelligent, well-groomed, capable of taking care of herself, and so out of place in the prison. My heart ached for her parents and child. Our society does not treat kindly the family of prisoners, especially those from the middle class. For the poor, survival is so difficult and being trounced by fate so normal that they do not care for society and its opinion. The rich are protected by their money, and in fact, notoriety may add to their status. But the middle class suffers from shame.

"You really think she is going to get bail?" I asked nobody in particular.

Shakira answered, "I doubt it. The case was well publicized. It seems she married a man much older than she. He was a rich businessman, some say an NRI (non-resident Indian). According to the media, he was first her employer and then he married her. One day he was found shot dead and completely naked lying in the gutter. She and another man, who she now claims is her husband, were arrested. I don't think she is going anywhere in a hurry."

I watched Vandana walk to her dormitory. It seemed unthinkable that she could be involved in such a gruesome crime. Only she really knew what actually took place on that fateful day. If she was innocent, may God help her gain her freedom.

Another prisoner was called and came to us. She was holding a baby who gaped at me in utter fascination. I asked about her history.

"Her name is Bimla. She is here, along with her mother, in a dowry case. The daughter-in-law of the house committed suicide. During that time, Bimla was at her mother's place. So she, along with her parents and her brother, was arrested."

I looked at Bimla. She smiled and came forward, and after gentle persuasion, she sat down on the vacant chair next to ours. She too had been in the old Gurgaon jail.

"That jail was very bad and not a place for children. This jail is a hundred times better, but I was hoping that there would be some school or activity for children. I have heard that Tihar jail is very good for children, as there is a nursery school where they are taught and taken good care of." She spoke in Hindi. Her voice was barely a whisper.

"Don't worry, these women are from India Vision Foundation, the same organization that is doing so much work for children in Tihar. They plan to start a nursery school for children here."

"Please, do it soon! Otherwise, the children pick up the bad habits of these prisoners. Also, if they spend all the time with their mothers, they do not learn to be independent, which is bad, as after a few years they have to live on their own. They will leave us and go. In my case, my child will have to go to an orphanage." Her voice was heavy with sadness and helplessness. "Please start something for the children. They should spend their time learning and playing, not being cooped up with us adults all the time." She then stood up, nodded, and left.

Getting By Inside

The third inmate we interviewed was the oldest—in her mid-forties. She had confidence in her stature and her eyes showed character and strength of will. God alone is aware of what she must have seen and endured.

"She is in prison for murdering her husband. She confessed her crime and is in for life. Her name is Revathy," Shakira told me as Revathy approached us. She sat down next to us and looked us in the eye.

"Were you also in the old Gurgaon prison?"

"No, I was in Hisar. I was there for seven years."

"How is this prison compared with that one?"

"There is no comparison. The one in Hisar is really excellent. The superintendent, Sashi Elahwat, is doing a wonderful job. There is work for women and a nursery school for the children. There is gardening, and we made money from the clothes we stitched and weaved."

"Were you treated well there?"

"It was a good prison. If the person in charge of the prison is decent, then automatically the prison becomes livable."

"In your opinion, how important is a nursery school for children in prison?"

"Most important. Otherwise they spend the entire day with criminals like us. Our language is not good. Our habits are not good. They pick up all the wrong habits in life. By the time they leave the prison, they are already set in their ways. If there is a nursery school, then at least the children spend six to seven hours with other children, playing and learning. By the time they come back to the cell, they are already tired. They spend some time with their mothers and then go to sleep. By the time they are five years old, they are capable of mixing with society and with outside children. Where work for us is concerned, like learning to weave and stitch as they teach in Tihar and in Hisar prisons, we women can earn money and help our families from inside the jail. Then when we get out of jail, we can continue to be employed. Also it passes our time." She spoke all this softly, calmly, in no particular hurry.

"You must be missing the friends you left behind in Hisar jail?"

She smiled.

"Life teaches you to accept every sorrow and joy that comes your way in an impersonal manner. Never get attached to anything. Attachment hurts in the end." She stood up and walked away. She was self-assured with a sagelike detachment in her eyes. You can meet philosophers in bars or prisons and find certified nut cases running empires and countries.

It was really hot now. The wind that touched my face felt as though it was from a furnace. I walked into the dormitory.

I noticed there were no fans. I shuddered at the thought of how they slept at night, especially the little children.

"Ruzbeh, you must meet this woman!" Shakira said.

I returned to my seat and saw a woman dressed as a yogi. In her arms she carried one of the cutest children I have ever seen. The woman, in her mid-forties, looked like a Spaniard. She was tall, thin, and had a certain poise that comes to those who are either spiritual or bone lazy. She belonged to the former category. She wore a saffron *lungi* (skirt) and *kurta* (shirt) with *Aum* printed on it. She smiled and for a minute or two played with the child. He eyed us all with a frown and then decided that we were not worthy of his attention. He put his big head on his mother's thin shoulder and shut his eyes. His chubby legs were riddled with mosquito bites, and off and on his fat fingers would caress these battle scars.

"Where are you from?"

"My name is Avia, and though I was born in Colombia, I have a Canadian passport." She spoke in a typical English accent.

"What have you done to get yourself and this little chap into prison?"

"I was set up by my so-called guru. He wanted me to discredit another swami. He asked me to claim that this child, Vishnu, was the swami's child, when in reality he is Vishnu's father. I have misplaced my documents, so he got somebody to complain about me and they put me in prison on the charge of illegal entry and domicile without possessing valid documents."

"Where is your family? Why don't they bail you out of this mess?"

She smiled and looked at her son, who smiled back at her, frowned at us, and then shut his eyes again.

"I just can't manage to disassociate myself from this

guru. He seems to have cast a spell on me. Even though I am aware that he is not a holy man and he is just using me, I can't seem to get out of his clutches. My eldest son is a priest in ISKCON (International Society for Krishna Consciousness) in Mumbai. My family wants to help me, but first they want me to disassociate myself from this man whom I call my guru. But I can't. So they are fed up with me and no longer want to be involved in my life." She smiled and shrugged her shoulders.

"If you know that man is a crook, then why don't you leave him and move on? You have this child now. You owe it to this boy."

"I know, but I can't move on. I am certain he has cast some spell on me. I have tried to get away, but I just can't." She smiled again helplessly. "That's what power in the hands of the wrong person can do. God help you if you get mesmerized by such a person."

Vishnu eyed us with distaste. He scratched his legs and looked at his mother.

"It's so hot inside that he can't sleep. And the flies! My God! I don't understand the other children. They can sleep with at least a hundred flies on them. This boy can't sleep with even one fly on him. So he stays awake and so do I. And some of these women are so dirty! They don't clean the toilets. They don't bother bathing. They speak and fight so loudly." She smiled and shrugged her thin shoulders. "But I guess one has to go through whatever destiny has in store for us. Destiny, God—it all means the same. I have a little money, so I can hire somebody to do work for me. At least that is a blessing."

If one has money, one can pay for work within the prison. Of course, if you have lots of money, then in all probability you will not get into prison, unless someone either richer or more powerful than you wants you in jail. During my conversations with numerous police officials, they told me about instances where a prisoner is switched with another person en route to prison from court. For example, Mr. A has committed a crime and has been convicted or has been caught committing a serious offense and is being taken to prison. On the way the cops switch Mr. A for somebody else. Either the substitute has been purchased to do the needful, or in some cases, when procurement of a quick substitute is not possible, the cops just pick up some poor homeless fellow, charge him with the offense, and substitute him for Mr. A. The poor fellow has no lawyer and nobody to speak to about his innocence. He might spend years imprisoned for somebody else's crime. It seems this modus operandi is particularly common in some states.

In prison, an inmate can buy services in various ways. You can have your clothes washed, your baby taken care of, prison work done for you, your body massaged, and you can assure your safety and security from lesbians and gangs operating within the cell. These services are provided in exchange for either cash or other services. One also needs money for basics like soap, medicine, food, cigarettes, matches, thread, needles, etc. And if you do not want to eat prison food, then money is a must.

Often, prison food is not palatable, so it is modified by adding spices. You are not supposed to possess chili powder in prison, but of course there are ways and means of getting it. Often, those prisoners who have money don't touch prison food. They order rations from outside and pay the poorer inmates to prepare a proper meal. The inmate is either paid in cash or can partake of the food. They cook makeshift traditional style. A few bricks are arranged in a square, within which either coal or *roti* (hard traditional bread) is used as fuel to light a fire and cook or heat food. Dinner is served by 5:30 (as in Yerwada jail). So the food is cold by nightfall. By sunset, the inmates are all locked up in their cells. So the food is normally heated in the cell itself. (I need to mention that a month later, I went back to Tihar jail, and the food I ate made by the women convicts for the inmates was outstanding. It was not only delicious but also nourishing.)

"Avia, when do you think you will be out of here?"

"A week. Maybe ten days. Not longer."

Four months later, she was still in prison. So was her son.

A World of Difference

I was fortunate to visit Gurgaon prison several times. Those visits enabled me to see what a world of difference an NGO, in this case, India Vision Foundation, can make inside a prison, especially for the children.

The first time I entered Gurgaon prison, there were absolutely no programs to improve the lives of the inmates and the children. The women sat gossiping, fighting, or sleeping. The children spent most of the time with their mothers in the cell. They were irritable and very much out of control. I returned a month later with the India Vision staff.

Summer was in full swing. The temperature was around 108°F and the hot wind made your skin want to fold up. I walked the familiar path to the barrack where India Vision Foundation had set up a weaving and stitching class as well as a small nursery school just opposite the barrack that housed the women. That barrack held 135 women (of which 114 were waiting for trial) and around 20 children. Of the three barracks, only one was occupied. Rather than use the two empty barracks, the administrator had decided to overcrowd the single barrack in use, since within a year all the barracks would be bursting at their concrete seams.

Entering the barrack, I heard the merry laughter of children at play. In the midst of a prison, hearing the sound of children enjoying themselves is an indescribable experience. Across from the nursery school, I saw women engrossed in learning to sew.

Sitting on mats, the children were busy drawing and coloring in their workbooks. A few children played with toys, and one child stood with hands on her hips, crying. She wanted her mother, who was at work in a mandatory job. Only the convicted have mandatory jobs. Those awaiting trial did not have to work in prison. One of the staff members took the child in her arms and distracted her with a stuffed doll. Charts of fruits, animals, and the alphabet hung on the wall. A few older children were seriously studying.

The children knew many of the India Vision Foundation staff members by name and each went to his or her favorite. It was obvious that the nursery school was already giving the children back their childhood. I was told that initially the nursery school would function for two to three hours a day until more funding was arranged to pay salaries for a full-day teacher and a helper. Compared with Tihar, this nursery was still in its infancy, but slowly and surely, social work achieves its objective.

A chubby young girl with a small ponytail and a rag doll in her hands approached me. Her name was Manisha.

"Harish took my plane. He is very bad. He hits all of us. You hit him."

I picked her up in my arms and approached the controversial Harish, who turned out to be a stocky boy, aptly nicknamed "Mike Tyson" by the India Vision Foundation staff.

"Will you please give Manisha her plane? She is crying and you don't want your friend to cry." He looked up at me, and perhaps deciding that he needed a few more years before disobeying me, nodded and quickly gave her the plane. The little girl shyly took the toy and offered young Tyson her doll. He looked at the doll, at the girl, and at me, then took the doll, threw it down, and picked up a broken car. He smiled at me, certain that I understood his anti-doll actions. Thereafter, whenever I visited the nursery school, he would quietly come and sit next to me.

Discarded toys light up the eyes of these children. For them, old and often broken toys are as precious as the stars in the sky.

"It's too hot in here. Don't you think we should insist on a fan for the children?" I asked.

"We have placed an application. They have promised they will install a fan for the children within a few days," said Shakira. "It takes time. We have asked a few of our sponsors to provide fans." (It took nearly a month and a half for the fan to be installed—twenty days for the fan, another twenty days for the electrical wiring.)

I walked to the opposite end of the barrack, where the stitching class was in progress. I was surprised to see them practicing by stitching on paper. The morning newspaper was never put to better use! Small frocks and dresses had been stitched from the paper.

"They practice on paper. When their hands are steady, they stitch on rough cloth. It is only when we are certain that they have learned well that we allow them to stitch on proper cloth. That goes for embroidery, too."

"Where is their work sold?"

"Mainly in the embassies. Also, some people place orders and then sell the garments abroad. Our Tihar projects took off like this—in such a humble way—but soon our articles were sold all over the world. In fact, many of our inmates had bank accounts for the first time and supported their families from inside the prison. It will happen here, too. All it needs is good management and support from sponsors."

The women were engrossed in learning their craft. They all worked without a word. Next I went to the residential barrack. Avia approached me with a broad smile. A month had gone by and she was still here.

"I thought you were leaving the prison."

"Yes, but what to do? There is some confusion over my documents. In a few days I shall be gone."

"How is it here? Have more fans arrived?"

"Just a few fans. Come let me show you around the dormitory." I walked in with her. There were four fans installed for 65 adults and 12 children in a dormitory that was at least a hundred feet in length. "It gets too hot, but what to do? This is a jail, not a five-star hotel. It is the dirtiness that gets to you. Take a look at the bathroom and toilets."

I had just inspected the bathrooms and toilets where the nursery was situated. They looked very clean. The contrast with this one shook me to the roots. I was met with the sight of thousands of flies. There was the stench of stale food, unwashed clothes, and urine. The bath area was clogged with dirty oily water.

"Why is there so much oil in the dirty water?"

"People cook food and then wash their dishes here. They not only wash their plates and pans here, but they don't bother to remove the scraps, so the leftover food goes down the drain and clogs it up. Also, most inmates lack basic sanitation and hygiene sense and are so dirty that it is really disgusting." I didn't linger because my lungs were screaming for air.

"I only wish there were more fans. The heat is really killing," Avia went on.

"Where's your son?"

"He is not well. He can't eat anything, and if he does, he can't keep it down. At the moment, he is sleeping under the fan. I have paid somebody to take care of him until

I finish my work. They get so jealous here that for a while, nobody was allowed to work for me. But in the end, there was a compromise, and now I can employ somebody to do my work." It sounded so strange, all this talk of employing people in prison, but life goes on with the survival of the fittest and the richest.

I saw Vandana cooking meals in the open space between the two dormitories. She wore pants and a blue shirt and looked like a college girl. She looked up but avoided my eyes. It was obvious that she would be here for years.

"She cooks three meals every day for her husband or her boyfriend and herself. Her man is in the male ward in this prison. She sends him food. Loves him a lot."

"I thought she had killed her husband."

"In prison, when a man and a woman inmate fall in love, they claim to be husband and wife because that allows them to meet once a week for half an hour. You can meet only with relatives or your spouse. So, if she claims to be his wife and he agrees, then they can meet once a week because nobody inquires about legal documents or proof of marriage."

Happy Children and Working Mothers

Two months later, I again visited Gurgaon prison. In the air-conditioned van that took me from the airport, a crying child reminded me of my little Mike Tyson, spending day and night in a stuffed dormitory, enduring the Delhi summer, now in full swing with the temperature as high as 111°F (44°C).

Back in Gurgaon prison, Shakira and another India Vision Foundation social worker brought two trunks of old clothes and toys for the children. Shakira and her friend looked at me and then at the trunks. It is universal. For all the talk about women's liberation and equality, when it comes to carrying a heavy load, all that talk is forgotten in a flash! So off they went, happily chatting about the joy these clothes and toys would bring to the children, while I carried the two trunks, grunting and sweating under a merciless sun.

Of course, the joy on the faces of the children when they saw the clothes, and especially the toys, made everything worthwhile. The clothes had been donated by well-wishers. Some were in great condition, and some were well worn, but that did not matter to the children. For them, the clothes were sent directly from paradise. The India Vision Foundation team began to match the clothes by size with the children. A red cap went to Vishnu, Avia's son. He beamed, smiling from ear to ear. No words can explain the joy in his eyes. Mike Tyson got a new shirt and gave me a shy smile. Manisha showed me her new T-shirt. Her best friend, Gaurav, showed me his blue cap. These little ones became my pals.

Just donate old clothes and toys. The joy this simple gesture brings to the underprivileged is astounding. It humbles you. It makes you realize how fortunate we are. Yet we still continue to complain about issues that are usually either self-created or just not worth the time and energy. Clothes, toys, crayons, books, slippers and shoes, towels and sheets—they can be passed on to so many who are really in need of them. I sat with the children for an hour or more. I saw them really excited, running to show their mothers the clothes and gifts they had received. I saw the mothers' eyes light up with joy on seeing their children so happy. I realized the importance of NGOs like India Vision Foundation, who reach out to give joy and solace, as well as a sense of well-being and dignity to the so-called underbelly of society.

Meanwhile, the fan was still not functional.

A month later, in early June, I once again visited the Gurgoan prison. Settling down with the children I realized that the heat was suffocating. I looked up and saw the fan but no wiring. Manisha came and sat by my side. She had a few pencils and crayons in her pudgy fingers. She wanted me to draw something, so I did.

"It is very hot. I am feeling very hot." She looked at me as if by my willing so, the fan would start working. Gaurav, with his perpetual blue cap, sat next to her. He smiled and drew in his drawing book. Mike Tyson came and sat down with a toy on which he put a small horse. He punched the horse. The toy went flying, and he looked at me and smiled. He did not speak much. His fist did the talking. I sat on the mat and sweated along with the children. Manisha moaned again and again that it was too hot.

"We'll try to get it repaired, okay?" I assured her.

"I want water." Manisha stood up and held my hand. Her two pals stood up, too.

Off we went in search of water. They took me to the bathroom, where they drank directly from the tap using metal cups provided by India Vision Foundation. For the next five minutes, I filled glass after glass. Either they were really thirsty or they liked the idea of me serving them water. Most of them drank so much that their little stomachs swelled up. We tromped back to the corridor and plopped down on the mats. A constable smiled and told me that it was too hot for children to be in prison.

"Where are you from?" I inquired.

"I was in the army. I live nearby. I spent fourteen years in the army. Army life is tough. This life is better. Yes, it gets boring, but at least I can spend time with my family. It is good of you all to come and serve these children and the women. I have seen other jails where life is so bad for

HIMALAYAN INSTITUTE PRESS
630 MAIN ST STE 350
HONESDALE PA 18431

Place
stamp
here

HIMALAYAN INSTITUTE™
P R E S S

www.HimalayanInstitute.org
1-800-822-4547

*"Every event regardless of how bitter and unpleasant
it may seem, is a direct expression of divine will,
and it contains the seeds of higher good."*

—PANDIT RAJMANI TIGUNAIT, PH.D.

Complete this card to receive a free catalog offering selections in spirituality, alter-
native healing, yoga, eastern philosophy, meditation, self-help and more.

PLEASE PRINT

Book in which this card was found:

_____

Name _____

Address _____

City, State, Zip _____

E-mail _____

050112

the children that it depresses you. We are poor people who have no say in the matter."

I was taken to the stitching class. One look at their work and it was obvious that huge strides had been made in the few weeks' interval since my last visit. Gone were the newspapers. They showed me lovely small pink frocks. The women had begun to do embroidery and had learned to weave complicated, beautiful designs.

"We received a donation of around 10,000 rupees, and out of that we bought raw material and hired a teacher. This will sustain us until they are capable of doing work that competes with the very best on the market. By then, with the grace of God, more donations will come through," Shakira explained.

One of the inmates spoke up, "Madam, we need to work more hours. Two hours are not enough." The other inmates nodded in agreement.

"We will make it a full day. Give us time." Shakira turned toward me. "At the moment, the funds only permit us to employ a teacher for two hours every day. Once the funds come through, we can have the teacher for the entire day. Then we can do so much more."

I knew the funds required were not huge. For a few thousand rupees (Rs1,000 = US$22.00), you could hire somebody to take care of either a nursery school or the stitching class. For both projects, the cost per month, along with raw materials, is around 10,000 rupees per month (about US$220.00). With these projects, children are educated, and the women learn a craft that enables them to be self-employed and support themselves and their families outside the prison. It is a win-win situation. All it needs is the compassion of the inspector general and the superintendent to allow NGOs like India Vision Foundation to function in the prison. If these three components—NGOs, funds, and compassion—are in place, life for the inmates and the children improves drastically.

"Please install a fan here. It is too hot to stitch and work in peace. Also the children are falling ill, and there is no doctor."

"What do you mean there is no doctor?" I inquired.

"There is no doctor. They had a doctor who was a pharmacist, but he died a month ago. Now they have another pharmacist, who is an inmate in the male ward, and he is substituting as the doctor."

"First of all, how can a pharmacist take the place of a doctor? Secondly, he is a man and it is mandatory to have a woman doctor for women and children inmates."

"Yes, but this is a new prison and things happen slowly."

"For six months these people have been without a decent qualified doctor. Let's meet with the welfare officer," I said.

"There is no welfare officer."

"Okay, does India Vision Foundation have a woman doctor who can visit them at least once a week?"

"We have asked the authorities for permission for our doctor to enter the prison, but it takes time. Come, let's visit the superintendent and ask permission again."

The superintendent was not in his office, so we met with Mr. Sharma, the deputy superintendent.

"Sir, first of all, the fan in our nursery school is not working. Secondly, we need to get a fan installed where the women are learning to stitch," said Shakira.

"It will be done today." I thought the man was talking through his hat, but the connection and the fans were installed that very day. One does come across officials who actually say what they mean and do what they say.

Shakira continued, "Sir, the women inmates and the children need a qualified woman doctor. We know that it might take time for an official assignment. In the meantime, is it possible for India Vision Foundation to bring its own homeopathic doctor to treat the inmates?"

"Make an application and we will grant the permission," Mr. Sharma promised.

Returning to my hotel room, I realized what a difference an NGO can make to the lives of those in prison. For instance, if the India Vision Foundation staff were not present, God alone knows when a qualified doctor would have entered that prison. A week later, official permission was granted to India Vision Foundation to bring in their homeopath to treat the women and children of Gurgaon prison. Two months later, the prison authorities appointed a woman doctor for the inmates.

The next time I visited the nursery school, there were two fans installed, and yes, both of them worked. Also, there was a fan in the stitching class, and yes, that one worked, too. God bless Mr. Sharma. The first thing Manisha said to me with a smile in her eyes was, "Now it is no longer so hot." Such a simple, matter-of-fact statement, yet I will happily carry it to my grave.

contrasts in orissa

PURI, IN THE STATE OF ORISSA, is a beautiful place. In eastern India, it is a noted pilgrimage site where Lord Jagannath (Krishna) and his family reside in a temple that one has to see to believe. To reach Puri, I flew into the airport at Bhubaneswar and rented a cab for the seventy-kilometer drive to Puri.

My cab driver, a round, unshaven, benign-looking man named Babu, smiled, revealing a perfect set of white teeth. He took me to his car and told me and the forty-odd bystanders that I was in safe hands. We took off, and four minutes later, I realized why the onlookers at the airport had looked at me with sympathy.

Babu suffered from a fanatical fascination with the horn. He honked at cars in front of our vehicle. He honked when there was no car in front of our vehicle. He even honked at speed breakers twenty meters away. He honked at a cyclist fifty feet away on the other side of the road. I knew I was in real trouble when he honked at a car waiting at the signal. The only time Babu did not use the horn was when two cars approaching us tried to overtake each other and we needed to warn the cyclists ahead of us.

Fortunately, the drive to Puri was beautiful. Farms were scattered everywhere and a cool breeze ruffled my hair. I saw children swinging on tree branches and playing happily, oblivious to the world. In spite of the prediction of a raging cyclone, it was a bright sunny day. When we reached Puri, Babu smiled and informed me that he was just a phone call away. I smiled, nodded, and assured him that I would never forget him.

By now it was nearing 4:00 p.m. I tried to grab a quick lunch. In every restaurant I got the same answer: "We no serve food till 6:00, sir. Lunchtime getting over by 2:00. No sir, no snack. One not eating between 2:00 and 6:00, sir. That's why it being called *rest*aurant." So I ate ice cream and walked to the police station. From there, I was taken on a scooter to the district jail of Puri.

A Pilgrimage to the District Jail of Puri

I saw the prison and my heart sank. I had seen many prisons, but this one was the smallest. We had been told that there were 20-odd children with their mothers in the Puri jail. I had my doubts.

Sunil Kumar Mohanty, superintendent of Puri jail, shook my hand.

"Why are you interested in children in prisons? There are hardly any children in prisons."

"Yerwada, in Pune, has around 20 children. Gurgaon, in Haryana, has 32 children, as of yesterday. Tihar, Delhi, has 25 as of last week."

"So many children in prison?" He looked at his staff. I could see he was perplexed. "How can family members allow a child to be locked up in prison?"

"Have you never encountered children in prison staying with their mothers?"

"I have. But never a group. One or two children for a short time. That's it. What kind of families would allow a child to be in prison? In Orissa, at least to my knowledge, it is rare to have so many children in prisons."

"When was the last time this prison had children staying with their mothers?"

"Let me see. Yes. A year ago, we had a child staying with her mother."

"For how long?"

"For a year and a half, but that is because there was nobody to take care of the child and the mother was going to be released anyway. If she was going to be here for a long time, I would have convinced her to put the child in an orphanage."

"Can I have a look at the women's ward?"

The gate opened for us and we walked into the main jail. It was actually a jail for men. It was nearing dusk. I saw various cottagelike barracks. It was dark inside and I was told that there was a regular shortage of power. The men lounged outside in the open. As we passed the barracks, I could sense the stagnation and lethargy. We walked along a wall and stopped in front of a small locked door. It was opened and we stepped into the women's ward. I saw a small dormitory in a state of semidarkness. A huge wall enclosed this dormitory from the outside world.

"How many women are lodged here at the moment?"

"Fifteen."

"What's the capacity of the ward?"

"Ten."

The women came out of their dismal dormitory, stood in line and joined their palms, in total subjection. It wasn't a *namaste* greeting. It was abject helplessness. From where I stood, flies and darkness greeted me. I could actually feel their sense of rejection and humiliation. The women were old. As they stood in that line with palms held together, it seemed as though they were praying to us. I turned around and walked out of the ward. How a child could have spent a year and a half in this hellhole without being scarred for life was beyond my comprehension. I tried to imagine how the child had lived with these women day after day, with no one to play with.

Back in the superintendent's office, I asked about NGO activities in the prison.

"The inmates are lazy. They don't want to learn anything. NGOs do try, but it is of no avail. Speaking about NGOs, there is one social organization that takes care of children whose mothers are in prison. It is next to the Bhubaneswar jail. In fact, they would be of some assistance to you. Go there tomorrow."

We spoke for a while longer.

"Thank God that in Orissa, though we may be a poor state, at least our sense of family bonding is very strong. I am being transferred to the Balasore jail; maybe India Vision Foundation can start something there for the women in prison. It is very important that women do work and learn a craft instead of just slowly dying everyday."

That night, after visiting the Jagannath Temple, my last thought before sleep embraced me was of those fifteen women, standing in line outside their miserable dormitory, palms joined, waiting either for a miracle or for death itself.

Poor, But Rich in Reforms

The management of the hotel in Bhubaneswar had a policy of awakening guests at periodic intervals until they gave up and admitted that sleep was out of the question. At around 6:00 a.m., the sudden shrill of the doorbell made me jump right out of bed. When my feet finally hit the floor, I tottered to the door, where a mug was thrust into my hands. It was still dark outside.

No sooner had I shut the door, put the mug on the table, and gone back to sleep, than again the bell rang. I thought someone wanted the mug back. So again I went to the door, only to have a second mug thrust into my hands.

"Sorry, sir, you already having your tea . . . ha ha . . ." It was too dark to see my tormenter. "Drink tea, sir. Good tea, sir."

I nodded and climbed back into bed. The air conditioning had gone out of control. I was certain it was way below zero. The bell rang again. This time I had the morning paper thrust into my hands.

"Sir, cyclone gone, God being great." I knew God was great but had never realized he had such a queer sense of humor. Thus, I was up and about two hours before the meeting with members of the Orissa Patita Udhar Samiti (OPUS). OPUS runs a home for prisoners' children situated on the ground floor of a bungalow barely a five-minute walk from the Bhubaneswar prison. The home is called Madhurmayee Adarsha Sikhya Niketan (MASN).

MASN is in a quiet by-lane. I was shown into the reception drawing room by Niraja Laxmi Mohapatra, the superintendent of MASN. She reminded me of Shenaz back in Yerwada jail—simple, dedicated, and exhausted. I could hear children singing *sa, re, ga*—the basics of Indian classical music. A harmonium, a man's soft, soothing voice, and then the gush of children, all trying their best to sing in tune, brought back memories of days gone by. I stood up and gestured to Niraja that I wanted to look inside.

There are three main rooms at MASN. Two are used for the boys, and the other for the girls. In the first room, fifteen boys and girls played carom (billiards), while others sat around giving advice. The room was airy but dark. As is often the case in Indian cities, the power had failed. The moment the children saw me, they stood up, rushed over, and touched my feet. It was such a heartwarming gesture that it brought tears to my eyes.

The musicians were in the other room. The teacher, a young man, was surrounded by boys and girls learning the rudiments of Indian classical music. I sat down for a while. So far away from home, it reminded me of what seemed like another lifetime, when I studied instrumental classical music.

Niraja told me that MASN was not even eight months

old and at the moment housed 37 children, 12 of which were girls. All the children were between the ages of five and eight. They all belonged to mothers who were convicted and imprisoned in thirteen jails in Orissa. OPUS conducted a survey that showed that there were around 200 children of convicted mothers who did not have anyplace to call home.

"We want to move into a bigger place, as there are so many children who need our help. But, we cannot do this on our own. We need financial support. We have received help from the government. Chief Minister Naveen Patnaik inaugurated our hostel; and the State Women and Child Development Department, with support from the state prison authorities, helped us get started."

I explained, "In Delhi, India Vision Foundation has a similar program where children whose mothers are in prison are given lodging, boarding, and education until graduation. Of course, the schools that accept and nurture the children play a vital role in integrating them with the mainstream. The children live at the school hostel on the premises. Social workers and nuns take care of them."

"We are doing something similar. But here in Bhubaneswar, there are no private schools with hostels that will keep our children. So we keep them with us and make sure that they go to a government-run school. At the moment they go to Jharapara Primary School. As there is a need to house more children, we are trying to work out funding through the government and generous donors, so we can rent bigger premises and eventually have a hostel building of our own in which many more children can stay, hopefully until they graduate."

The children have a strict routine. On school days, they wake up at 5:00 a.m. and say their prayers for half an hour. They practice yoga and exercise for half an hour before breakfast at 6:30. From 7:00 to 8:30 they complete their homework. Then they bathe. At 9:15, they have lunch. Yes, at 9:15 they have lunch! From 10:00 to 4:00, they are at school. At 4:30, they go to a park adjacent to the prison and play. At 6:30 p.m. there is prayer and moral cultural education time. (That could mean singing Indian classical music or learning a musical instrument. It could also mean being bored to death listening to a lecture on morality and code of conduct.) From 6:45 to 9:15, they study. Then it is dinnertime. Lights are off at 10:00 p.m.

During vacation time, they study from 7:00 to 11:00 a.m., have their lunch, rest for two hours in the afternoon, and then go back to their books until 4:00 p.m. The rest of the schedule remains the same. They still get up at 5:00 a.m. and go to bed by 10:00 p.m.

All the children had a few things in common. They had spent some part of their lives in prison. They had mothers in jail, and it would be many years before they were united as a normal family. Initially, their smiles did not reach their eyes, but as they got to know me, they began to trust me as a friend. Life for most of them could not have been easy. It still was no bed of roses. They had to behave in a certain manner that fitted into the scheme of things. Like cogs in a wheel, they had to adhere to rules and regulations. Though children, they had to behave far more responsibly and act more mature than their age. My own two children created more pandemonium than all of them put together. Of course, most of them know how fortunate they are to have this small social organization to keep them safe and secure.

Neerja and I then went to the Bhubaneswar prison. It is just a five-minute walk from their hostel. The prison gates opened and I met the jail superintendent, Basant Kumar Ojha. Speaking to him, I realized what a difference an individual can make in an institution, especially in an establishment where sorrow and misery are not exceptions but the rule.

"Orissa may be one of the poorest states in the country, but I can assure you that what is happening within Bhubaneswar prison is extraordinary. Did you know that two years ago, for the first time in India, we made certain that two children living in this prison were allowed to go to school every day? Though the government does not have any provisions for allowing children of jail inmates to go to school, we were eager to start this program and are so happy that it is a success. Both of the children are still here and they go to school every day. It's thanks to OPUS that this venture is a success. They stepped in and not only made sure that the children were admitted to Vidya Mandir School but also assumed all the expenses themselves, from schoolbooks to uniforms to fees. We need social organizations like these to make a difference. It was Dr. Kiran Bedi's initiatives that convinced us all that reforms are not only possible but should be the rule in every prison."

Later on, we entered the main Bhubaneswar prison. It was an eye-opener. The prison was a vast acreage that looked like a garden. Although it looked natural, somebody had taken pains to beautify the place. Trees, shrubs, and bushes dotted the landscape. There were numerous temples within the prison itself, all constructed by the inmates. The superintendent told me that there was also a place constructed for Muslim worshipers. The women's ward was within the prison, and just like the Puri district prison, their dormitory was cordoned off by a huge wall. The similarities ended there.

The dormitory had two quarters occupied by 28 women and two children. The actual capacity was 14, but the women had meticulously maintained the place, so the overcrowding was not so apparent. Both the children went to the nearby school each day, and they seemed happy and at ease among our small crowd of observers. The quarters were clean and equipped with fans and a television set. The women went about their work and seemed far less miserable than most of the women inmates in other prisons. Next to their quarters stood a dilapidated cottage, which obviously had been vacant a long time.

"If we had some kind of funding, we could use this place for some constructive purpose. We need help from organizations and NGOs to start self-employment programs. Sometimes, there is a desire to learn and work, but with a lack of funding and dearth of professionals working with the prisoners, nothing constructive takes place. Even individuals can make a huge difference in the lives of the underprivileged. Of course, if corporations help out, nothing could be better."

Bhubaneswar prison made me realize just how much depended on the compassion of the administration and the mental attitude of the prisoners themselves. In one of the poorest states in the country, Bhubaneswar prison was rich in reforms, initiatives, and compassion.

In the evening, I returned to MASN. It was around 4:30 p.m. and I wanted to join the children for playtime in the park adjacent to the prison. The staff of four dedicated women helped the children get dressed. There was a sense of excitement. They all got in line. Their hair was brushed and their faces scrubbed. Their clothes were well ironed and clean.

In the park some played on the slides and seesaws, while some sat and quietly looked on. I saw one child limping and was told that this child had been living on the street, begging. When they brought him to MASN, he could not walk and had to drag himself on the floor. It had taken MASN six months of medical aid and a good diet to heal the child so he could run with only a slight limp.

"This limp too will go away. All the children need is love, care, and protection. As long as we are around, they will get it."

I stared at the child playing with his friends. He looked back at us, waved, and smiled. My heart melted.

in the wrong place
at the wrong time

.

TIME WAS RUNNING OUT. I wanted to end my visits to prisons with a journey to Kashmir. There were two reasons. Kashmir has always fascinated me. To live in one of the most beautiful places in the world and be surrounded by constant hostility and violence was a heartwrenching paradox. The second reason was a chance meeting with Mr. G. N. Var.

Mr. Var, a thin, bearded man with a radiant smile and nerves of steel, was arrested in New Delhi in 1993. Being a Kashmiri Muslim in the wrong place at the wrong time was good enough for the authorities to book him under TADA (Terrorist and Detention Act). It took the government seven years to realize that he was innocent.

While in Tihar jail, Mr. Var completed a master's degree in management and business administration. He now offered to take me to Kashmir.

"You wanted to go to Kashmir to visit a prison. As Providence would have it, I am flying tomorrow. Let's go together."

After a while, he told me the story of his life in Tihar jail.

A Kashmiri in Tihar Jail

"I am from Kashmir, from an affluent family. In August 1993 I came to Delhi on business. On August 15, Independence Day, many Kashmiris, including me, were arrested by some corrupt officers of the Delhi Police, mainly to extort money from us. I argued with those police officials and paid an extremely dear price. They booked me under the terrorist act, and I was sent to Tihar jail in October 1993.

"When I entered Tihar, many Kashmiris were waiting to receive me. They told me that fortunately Dr. Kiran Bedi, the inspector general, had converted a hellhole into a virtual ashram. Otherwise the prison would have been hell for me. They briefed me about the prison way of life and gave me coupons worth 500 rupees. They explained how to use the coupons, how to purchase personal items from the canteen, how to pay 100 rupees to the head warden and 50 rupees to the ward *munshi* (usually a convict), to keep them in good humor and to avoid being given menial jobs such as cleaning the toilets.

"After a few days, I saw a petition box. I silently dropped a complaint. After three days, Madam Bedi visited the ward. As she entered, I saw a wave of joy among the inmates. She asked if we had any problems. Being newcomers we kept quiet. However, without pointing to anybody in particular, she directed the superintendent accompanying her to ensure that the newcomers were not harassed.

"As the days passed, I tried to cope with this unexpected situation and face the onslaughts of destiny with a smiling face. You can't imagine how humiliating and frustrating it is to be put behind bars through no fault of your own—to be jailed just because you happen to be from Kashmir. It was difficult to hide the mental agony. The brutal police torture, the post-arrest mental trauma, the mechanical and inhuman judiciary, the long separation from family and friends, the emotional breakdown—all this was bad enough, but to spend life behind bars was the biggest punishment. Who did this to me, and why did they do it? These were issues eating into my very soul.

"At this difficult juncture, the most painful period of my life, I saw Kiran Bedi in various roles: as a loving mother, an affectionate teacher, an able administrator, a determined reformer, an innovative researcher, and a remarkable visionary. Each time she visited the jail, she gave us new ideas, new directions and instructions, and ensured that the rules were followed properly in letter and in spirit.

She transformed the prison into a university with a difference. 'Help thyself—reformation through education' became the slogan. The India Gandhi National Open University (IGNOU) began in prison. We enrolled students in various courses. I became a teacher and was given much respect. That was what saved me from turning into a bitter and negative person.

"But as so often happens, happiness is short-lived. We received news of Madam Bedi's transfer. There was an outcry in the prison. Tears rolled down the cheeks of hard-core criminals. Many prisoners refused to eat.

"That evening, I was called in by the deputy superintendent, who threatened, 'Madam Bedi's days are over. We have reports that you are an instigator. Mind your own business, or you will suffer the consequences.' Despite threats we went on a hunger strike, venting our feelings peacefully.

"A few days passed and the new inspector general warned us, 'This is a jail. Forget Kiran's ashram and behave.' After a few weeks, the selective punishment started. The reformation process initiated by Madam Bedi was gradually stopped. I was sent to the punishment ward. My movement was restricted. Many times I was humiliated. My friends and I wrote to various ministries, human rights organizations, embassies, courts, and to people in positions of power.

"Responses started to pour in and the teams of various human rights groups, such as the Red Cross and the embassies, demanded explanations from the prison authorities. A few weeks later, a warden came to me saying, 'Pack your belongings, you are being moved.' He took me to the hospital ward. I really didn't know what was happening. Then it struck me. They wanted to prove that I was not of sound mind and thus not in my senses while making observations about the torture and brutality taking place in the prison.

"My apprehensions proved correct. I was admitted to

the psychiatric ward for inmates of unsound mind. I asked to meet with the superintendent or the deputy superintendent but to no avail. I argued with the head warden and told him, "Look, I will file a case against you and then the superintendent won't be able to help you. Show me the reason for this. You know that I am not mentally unbalanced. Don't put me with these people!" The head warden expressed his helplessness and said that the orders were from headquarters. Later on I found out that the administration had written to various organizations saying that I was mentally imbalanced and under psychiatric treatment, and thus my observations were not to be taken seriously.

"Life with insane inmates was hell. It was the biggest punishment. I really feared for my life and safety. I could have been murdered and no one would have noticed or cared. Who cares if an insane prisoner murders another insane prison inmate? I could not sleep at night for fear I would be strangled or viciously attacked. Nor could I take regular baths. I remember I took my first bath after fifteen days. I remained in this situation for three months. Those certainly were the worst days of my life. After three long months, the superintendent suddenly called me to his office and said, 'You have caused trouble for the inspector general. I hope you have realized that no good will come your way. We have transferred you back to the IGNOU Ward. Go and teach there.'

"And so I moved back to Ward No. 2 and began to teach again. Since education in prison—particularly the IGNOU program—had much publicity, the administration could not afford to earn a bad name by closing it down. Moreover, Madam Bedi by then had taken over as the special secretary to the lieutenant governor of Delhi, and the governor's office had started seeking explanations from the prison administration on various issues.

"About that time, Dr. D. C. Saxena, chairman of the Department of English, Punjab University, was convicted for contempt of court for filing a petition against the then chief justice of India. Dr. Saxena, a living legend, is a symbol of absolute honesty, integrity, and indelible character. He is a one-man army and a great crusader against corruption in the judiciary and in education. This imprisonment was a blessing in disguise, for he was a source of inspiration to all of us. He was instrumental in establishing a large library in the jail. He also started classes for civil services competitions.

"After the release of Dr. Saxena, things once again changed from bad to worse. Some inmates were peddling heroin in the IGNOU Ward in collaboration with the prison staff. I resisted but the drug mafia had the blessings of the staff. One day, after teaching at IGNOU, I was brutally assaulted by a warden known for supplying smack. I was admitted to the hospital in critical condition. Although the superintendent reprimanded the warden, for me it was nothing but lip service.

"In the meantime, a fictitious report was published in the newspapers that 'terrorists were planning to attack the jail.' This was a good excuse for the inspector general to once again persecute me. I was told that in accordance with the government I was being transferred to the high-risk ward.

"Life in the high-security ward of Jail 2 was again tough. I wrote to various authorities, but nobody was willing to come to the defense of a Kashmiri Muslim. It took seven years to win my case. I was honorably released in 1999. Hundreds of thousands of rupees had been spent on my case. My father had died a heartbroken man while I was in jail. A very big part of me wanted to seek revenge on all those who had put me in such a miserable situation. I had lost seven precious years of my youth. Much money was wasted. My family and friends were put through so much heartache. Why? Yes, there are militants in Kashmir. There are antisocial and antinational elements. But to assume every Kashmiri is an antisocial, antinational militant was not only offensive but also was against the very principles of all that is noble and good.

"The day I landed back in Kashmir, I tried to set a good example, like Dr. Bedi and Dr. Saxena. I tried to forget all the ordeals I had suffered in prison. I tried to console myself and prayed to God to help me. Despite chaos and confusion in the political scenario, I was advised to join a political party if I wanted a long and hassle-free life. The parties were suffering from inherent confusion and I did not want anything to do with politicians. I was under surveillance for a long time. But time passed, and finally everyone got the message clearly. I wanted to heal—not hurt—others.

"I am obsessed by my own mission—bringing about a social and economic reform in the Kashmir valley. I began an NGO and named it the Dr. Saxena Vision Foundation. This NGO established a quality educational institution that provides coaching for civil service aspirants. Recently the college was in the news for the remarkable achievements of its students.

"Then fate struck again. All my efforts in this direction suffered a setback when the institution's building was gutted by fire. It was a big blow to my aspirations. I could not withstand the irreparable loss. Books, furniture, and equipment worth ten and a half million rupees (US$330,000) were heaped in ruins in the rubble of my institution. No one came to my rescue.

"But I knew the show must go on. After enduring seven years in Tihar and not turning bitter, I did not intend to let anything get in my way or stop me from serving society. I know the common misconception is that a Muslim Kashmiri is a militant by nature. I know for sure that most of my Kashmiri brothers and sisters are just trying to live life with dignity. So many of my friends from Tihar, who were falsely imprisoned and years later released, are serving society now, and most of them are either Muslims or Kashmiri Muslims. Instead of becoming bitter and negative, we have turned more humane and conscious of living up to the image of our mentors, Dr. Kiran Bedi and Dr. Saxena. We don't intend to let them down."

Caught Between the Military and the Militants

Mr. Var met me at the Srinagar airport. Driving through the quaint lanes of Srinagar, it is hard to believe that this is the abode of militancy and of so much bloodshed. The ordinary man who just wants to live life peacefully with self-respect and dignity is caught in the crossfire between the militants with their own agenda and the military police and the local government. The average citizen lives with silent resignation and perpetual fear. Girls as young as four and women as old as eighty have been raped. The militants as well as the military and police are regarded with suspicion, fear, and hatred.

From my few days' stay in Srinagar, it appeared to me that for the Kashmiri people, no cost is too high, no trouble too daunting, no sacrifice too great, to make certain that their children are educated. The number of Kashmiris I personally met who have doctorates made my head spin.

Dr. Lone, the superintendent of Srinagar prison, has a Ph.D. in psychology. He told me, "The average man wants his children to be educated and not only be prosperous but also serve the community at large. Parents will go to any length to make certain that their children get a good education. That is why you will not find many children in our prisons. The mother will not mind the child staying in an orphanage or with relatives as long as the child's education does not suffer. Even though the child may be miserable with uncaring relatives, or the orphanage may be horrible, as long as the child is being educated, the mother does not want anything more. Consider this. There are no children here. It's not that women inmates don't have small children and don't want to spend time with them. The reason is that they don't want their child to grow up with other prisoners and miss an education. I often feel a child is far safer in prison with his mother than in the outside world. For example, young girls are lured into the wrong trade or become informants of militants, the military, or the police. Once they become informants, their lives become a living hell, because to make one group happy, you end up displeasing the other groups. They are caught in the crossfire. Nevertheless, the mother would prefer the child to be outside the prison, where at least there is a possibility that the child will be educated.

"I will give you an example. Just yesterday, a young girl of twelve was brought to me. Her mother is in jail. The girl has no place to go. The orphanage wants her out, for a reason known only to them. The mother and child are in prison. The mother does not know what to do with her daughter, as the daughter cannot be kept here for long. I can let her be here for one week at the most."

He then rang the bell and called for the mother and child. A few minutes later, they entered. The mother seemed to carry the weight of the universe on her bent shoulders. In the mother's eyes was so much fear and anxiety that it was hard to look at her. The reason was obvious. The daughter looked far older than her age. To have a mature girl all alone in the world at the mercy of society is a parent's worst nightmare.

"Isn't there anyone she can send the child to?" I asked

Mr. Var, who served as our interpreter.

"She says that there is nobody. A few relatives, but they cannot be trusted."

"No good orphanages?"

"Most of them are not good or safe, and it takes time to get admission. Time is one thing we don't have."

"Can't she stay here till something works out?"

Dr. Lone answered, "I can let her stay for a week or maybe two weeks, but no longer. She is above the age of five but still a minor. The crux of the problem is that neither the relatives nor the orphanages are safe."

The mother was silent. Her body language spoke of stress, helplessness, and defeat. The poor girl kept twisting her fingers and looking down at the floor. She was twelve years old, nearly my daughter's age. The thought made me shudder.

"Sometime back I was told a similar story by a friend of mine," Dr. Lone said. "This friend, Akbar, spoke about a young girl by the name of Jameela. Her father had disappeared some time ago, leaving the girl, her brother, and her mother to fend for themselves with no money or source of income. Two years ago, her mother was kidnapped, leaving the children all alone. After fifteen days or so, the mother returned with a new husband, the man who had kidnapped her. All was well for a while, until both the stepfather and mother were picked up for some crime.

"Then, according to my friend, the stepfather's brother took both of the children to his house. The boy was sent to work in the market, selling fruit all day, and the money went to the uncle, who said that he needed the cash for the lawyer's fees to get the parents out of prison. The girl did the housework—washing clothes, sweeping the house, and cooking food. There was no chance of their education continuing. The girl grew weak and thinner by the day. This friend of mine somehow got the children out of the house and admitted the girl to an orphanage. The boy, slightly older, went to live with some friends. They worked all day and night to feed themselves and pay the rent. Just last week, my friend told me that the orphanage had expelled the girl. He has somehow found temporary shelter for her, but for how long is the question. God alone knows what will happen to the child. There are innumerable cases like these."

We went to visit the women's ward. It was more like two cottages surrounded by a high wall. Initially there had been one cottage, with a small room to lodge seven to nine inmates. The other cottage was slightly bigger, and on that day there were twenty-two inmates, most of whom were waiting for trial. The cottages were clean and had carpet on the floor. The women were given rations and they cooked their own food. They ranged in age from nineteen to more than sixty, but not one looked like a criminal or a militant. The cottages were well kept, and each woman had been allocated a small space where her bag and clothes were kept. The women wore what they possessed, not any particular uniform. Many wore a large robe draped over their *salwar-kameez*.

I walked around the cottages. You can see the beautiful mountains so clearly. I thought how painful it must be to be caged up in a small place when the sky and mountains beckon. I saw a young girl studying outside the cottage in a secluded spot. She could not have been more than twenty years old. She was sitting on the grass with her back to the cottage wall. I noticed that she was learning to write in English. She had written the words *one hundred and nine* and *one hundred and ten* neatly in a column to the end of the page. There were other books beside her, all in Urdu. Her pencil was nothing but a stub. I asked who taught her in prison, but she obviously could not understand, so she smiled and nodded.

"That girl studying there is a militant," one of the security personnel explained. I turned and looked at her again as she grappled with the English language. I could not imagine a gun in her hand instead of the stubby pencil.

The next day, we were back in the prison. I wanted to spend time alone with the inmates. I had Mr. Var with me, and Dr. Lone allowed us to sit with the inmates without the presence of security guards. His confidence in us spoke highly of him as an officer and a human being.

We sat in the small room of the old cottage. I first met the mother with whom I had spoken the day before. She had sent her daughter to a friend's home. Mr. Var once again played the role of translator.

"You sent her to a friend's house. How safe is she?"

"As safe as she can be. I have no option. Until she can go to the orphanage, she will have to remain there. God will take care of her."

I nodded. God for sure had lots to take care of in Kashmir. I then asked if we could find a good orphanage for her daughter. Mr. Var had spoken to Dr. Bedi and her daughter, Saina, and they were eager to start a home for abandoned children in Kashmir. The woman looked at me for a long time. She then nodded affirmatively.

"If she starts something in Kashmir, then yes, I can trust my daughter with her. But I am so frightened for my daughter's future now. I don't know what to do." She had tears in her eyes. I looked down at the carpet on which we sat. I did not have the solution. I wished there was something I could do for her. I hoped that there could be organizations run by decent social workers for the welfare of children in every city and town. Pakistan and India spend millions of rupees keeping the flame of hatred alive in Kashmir. If only one of them decided that the surest way to win public support was through social work and taking care of the women and children, Kashmir would be theirs for the asking. It seems that serving the poor and the down-trodden is way down on the list of their priorities.

Next, a woman in her mid-thirties or early forties entered. She was extremely fair and had the typical features of Kashmiris—a long and clear visage, a soft voice, and a natural tendency to be polite. I asked her what her problem was. She began to speak, and though I did not understand a word, the pain in her eyes and the tears rushing down her cheeks told a familiar story.

She had been in prison for the last three years. She had four children. When she was imprisoned, her youngest child was two years old and the oldest was twelve. She did not know where they were now. They moved about from relative to relative because she was from an affluent family, and they wanted to squeeze the last rupee out of her.

"When was the last time you saw your children?"

"I have not seen them since I was put in prison." Tears ran down her face.

"Why didn't you bring the two-year-old with you to the prison?"

"I tried, but I could not manage. Sometimes the judge was not present. Sometimes there was nobody to go to my hometown to get the child. Sometimes my lawyer was not present. Sometimes the other party's lawyer was not present."

The bottom line is that for three years, this mother did not have her child with her as a result of apathy and ineptness on the part of the prison authorities, judiciary, and welfare officer. She sat and wept. Two of her friends sat beside her and tried to console her.

Another inmate spoke to me in Hindi, "Just let her meet with her children. After that, at least her heart will be light. Now there is no word, no letter—nothing from them. She does not know how and where they are. Only this much is known: they are staying with assorted family members."

I spoke to Mr. Var. He promised to bring up the case with a few lawyer friends to see what could be done. India Vision Foundation should immediately begin a Kashmir chapter, he suggested. There certainly is a need for it in Kashmir.

Her friend went on, "She does not have any clothes. We help her. The fellow women inmates share their clothes with those women who have nobody to care about them. Please do something. She cries so much that it breaks our hearts."

I could not bear to look at her, this woman who had not seen her children for three years. As our legal system fell short of delivering justice, I felt equally responsible. When one's country fails to even try to fulfill its obligations to its citizens, then we as citizens are equally responsible in the failure.

The next inmate wept even before a single question was asked. Her story summed up the plight of so many Kashmiri people. She was an informant of the military. She did not want to be an informant, but she had no option. In Kashmir, I was told, the police and the military did not see eye to eye. Thus, if you were an informant to one, you were automatically an enemy to the other. This woman was caught between the two.

"Brother, I have done nothing wrong. I was sitting at a tea stall, having tea, when the police arrested me for loitering and put me behind bars. My child is now with my husband, who is a drug addict. Please, get my child to me. Please! My husband will do anything for drugs. I am frightened for my child."

"Why didn't you tell the judge that you are innocent and that you want your child with you?"

"They have not taken me to any judge. I have been in prison since they took me from that tea stall."

"How is that possible? You must appear in front of a judge within twenty-four hours of being arrested." According to our constitution, each individual arrested by the police has the right to appear before a magistrate within twenty-four hours of the arrest. This is our constitutional right. And here in front of me sat a woman who had been imprisoned for seven days without seeing the outside of the prison cell, let alone been presented to a magistrate.

"Please, just help me to bring my child here. I do not want to appear before a judge. I just want my child. I really am innocent. I am not a bad woman. I have been framed by the police. I had no option. If I did not help the military, then they would have harassed me; if not the military, then the police; and if neither, then the militants. What is one to do? Please, help me. Bring my child to me."

She sat and wept. Mr. Var explained that there were innumerable cases where people disappeared, never to resurface. The militants, the military, the police, the intelligence agencies, and, often, personal enmity—all were reasons enough. At first, I thought that Mr. Var was prejudiced against anything that had the stamp of the Indian Government. But late that night I met with a journalist who came from a lineage of orthodox Brahmin Hindus. When I asked his viewpoint on the happenings in Kashmir, his observations were very similar to those made by Mr. Var.

"Two of my colleagues wrote a few strong articles against the military. Both of them have disappeared. It's been twenty-three days. There is no news of them. Most militants are bastards, but unfortunately, the military is not far behind. I am not saying that all those in the military are bad, but there is a faction that is just horrible. I am Indian through and through, but I tell you both the militants and the military have played an equally ruthless role in creating so much misery and sorrow in the lives of the common Kashmiri."

So I sat in front of this woman and watched her weep. Then two women lifted her gently and took her out. Minutes later, another group of women entered. I was told that they all belonged to one family—a mother and four daughters, ranging in age from nineteen to twenty-four. They had been here for the last seven months.

They were booked for murder. It was a family dispute. One night, during a fight, a man died. The mother claimed self-defense, but the entire family was booked for murder. It appeared that someone had paid money to put these women behind bars. All the women wanted was a lawyer to represent them. Nobody seemed to be paying any attention to them, and if things continued, they would spend years behind bars before their matter even reached the court.

The young woman accused of being a militant came in next and sat down near the other women. Mr. Var translated her story. She lived with her two sisters and her mentally challenged father. One day, the militants approached her to become their informant. She tried to refuse, but she was well aware of the consequences to herself and her sisters if she did. So she reluctantly agreed. When the military found out, they forced her to work for them. Once again, she had little say in the matter. Sometime later the militants realized that she had betrayed them. They threatened her with dire consequences, and thus she became a double informant. One day she was caught supplying information to the militants, and she was imprisoned. She was not worried about herself, but she was worried about her young sisters, one fourteen and the other eighteen, and about her mentally challenged father. All she wanted was for someone to help her sisters get to a rehabilitation home and to institutionalize her father. She had no other desire.

I left the prison with a heavy heart. Not even the mountains could lift my spirit.

the power of compassion

I WAITED FOR DR. KIRAN BEDI in her office adjacent to her bungalow. Security was expecting me, and my business card was enough to let me enter the quaint garden around the small cottage that doubled as an office. India Vision Foundation operates from two cottages adjacent to the residential quarters.

After a short wait, Dr. Bedi arrived. She was in a rush because she was due to leave in a few days for a post with the United Nations as the civilian police advisor in the Department of Peace-Keeping Operations. As we headed for the house, a security officer introduced her to a young man who was either a relative or close friend of the security officer, and who wanted a job in some government department. Dr. Bedi listened to his request and then turned to her security guard.

"Shall I tell you the truth or just make you feel happy? You decide. If you want the truth, the fact is that there is no way he can get the job that he is asking for. Forget me. Nobody can get him this job. If I were a politician, I would have told you that I will try my best and to leave his bio-data. Fortunately for both of us, I am not a politician, so I am going to be forthright. Forget trying for this job. If I can help you in any other way, let me know."

She led the way into the drawing room. We sat down on comfortable sofas.

As we were about to start, a family member came in to wish her bon voyage. Dr. Bedi excused herself, hugged her aunt, and assured her that no matter where she was in the world, her family was always with her in mind and spirit. Behind her on the wall was a picture of Sai Baba of Shirdi, looking all warm and snug in his laminated frame, and there I was, shivering—cursing Delhi, the rain, the fog, and Tihar—chilled to the marrow of my bones. Someone must have felt sorry for me, because a tray of hot tea magically appeared.

Getting the Community Involved

"Let's start," said the tough-as-nails Kiran Bedi.

"In your book, *It's Always Possible,* you have described in great detail the pathetic conditions that existed in Tihar jail when you took over. Are there currently any jails in India that resemble Tihar at that time?"

"By and large, I think all."

"You mean that the inhumane conditions that existed in Tihar are still rampant in jails all over the country?"

"Absolutely. You must understand that after seeing the revolutionary changes in Tihar since 1993, a lot of jails have made progress. But what worries me the most is the lack of humaneness and that there is no coordinated holistic approach. Most jails are not run on the town model. If you have buildings in a town but don't have anyone to clean them or supervise them, it leads to major health problems. Or, say you have a town without a police station, or you don't have a court, or you don't have a health center, or dispensary, or you don't have a school—then that is not a town. A town means having these things. It's the job of the town commissioner and the town mayor to see that the town has all the basic necessities required for a comfortable life. You don't have to migrate somewhere else if your own town provides you with all these amenities and opportunities. Tihar has become like a town. Tihar has everything required by different sections of the jail society. Because we made Tihar into a town, it has worked wonderfully.

"I asked the community for the things that we didn't have in our government budget. Every time a social worker or an NGO enters Tihar—or any jail for that matter—the prison security clears them. They are given an ID card and frisked when they enter. So where is the problem? Also, the most important thing was that I had nothing to hide.

There is total transparency here. I believe that if you are serving the people, then their representatives have a right to know things. Thus, we started practicing 'the right to know' in 1993. Prisoners have the right to know and citizens have the right to know what is happening in their prison and how we are treating prisoners. Every prisoner has the right to know 'what am I entitled to' and 'what can I ask for?'

"The second thing that I insisted upon was community participation. The community does not have the right to enter the prison, but as the inspector general of Tihar jail, I used my discretion to allow NGOs and those who can serve the prisoners in Tihar."

Dr. Bedi set a precedent by opening the doors of Tihar to the media and social organizations. Until then, not only in Tihar but also throughout the country, prison authorities did their best to maintain a shroud of secrecy around what happened behind the massive iron gates.

"The prison manual gives the power of discretion to the inspector general and to the prison superintendent to give the community access to the prison. There is the right of discretion in every job. The problem is most prison authorities use their discretion to reject, rather than facilitate, the help that is offered. Why? Because rejection is simple; one word and the matter is closed. But giving permission for help means you have to supervise, then follow up; then you have some corrections to make. Later you may have to make some additions, then you have to respond, and, finally, provide. So, often, those in charge say, 'What a nuisance. What is the need?' and they reject the help. What most of them do not understand is why we are here. We are here to make certain that the prisoner will never come back. To 'reform' the prisoner so he or she will never again resort to crime.

"I decided that I was responsible for the prisoners and their welfare, and I decided to create a township. They became my focus. The women became my focus. Their children became my focus. If anybody objected, I would ask, 'What's the problem?' Every town has a mayor. If they are good mayors, then they will look at every angle of a citizen's rights. Let us look at the children. Are they going out? All right, they are staying with their mothers because there is no security outside. But then, they needn't be jailed. They could go in and out. They can come home at night—home meaning they can come back to their mothers at night. Let this become a home, rather than a prison. Take them out. Let them study. Let them go to a nearby nursery—and that is what we started to do.

"I had no money. But that does not mean we did not have resources. I cashed in all the goodwill I had. I had been to many schools and colleges as a police officer in Delhi. I called all my friends who were principals and told them, 'Now is the time for you all to help me. Give me all your old books. Give me your old clothes. Give me school supplies.' This could have cost the government hundreds of thousands of rupees and would never have made it in the budget. So I asked, 'Give me teachers, give me language teachers, give me buses. I want to move the children in and out.' Even health care came through the community."

Let the Children Out of Prison

Dr. Bedi continued, "What I am saying is allow NGOs to enter the prisons. They want to help. They are pleading to help. Let them in. In fact, there are innumerable good government programs. My social organization, India Vision Foundation, also runs through government programs. The nursery is totally government supported. We are the only ones who have this program in the prison. Why can't others follow? Approach the Central Social Welfare Board and get something out of it. What the government gives us meets 25 percent of our total cost. To meet our entire cost we have to raise funds. The point is, every inspector general and every superintendent of a prison has the right and the capacity to ask the community to help. There are NGOs waiting at the door, willing to help you. India is full of good NGOs. India is full of women with time on their hands, and they would love to come forward and help the underprivileged, especially children.

"I personally think every prison has the capacity to run a nursery—and run nursery training programs for women. There must be a nursery school for children, even if there are just four or five children in the prison."

"Should this be compulsory?" I asked.

"Yes. You must also understand that all this can be made possible only if there is healthy interaction with NGOs. The number of children we have in Tihar is phenomenal. Nowhere in any other jail in India are there as many children as in Tihar. It means that nowhere else can any inspector general claim that providing a nursery is too big a problem. Tihar has the biggest problems, and we have found a solution. It means in other jails the problem is smaller and there should be an easier solution. Why should there be any problem in any other jail in our country? There must be a nursery school inside prisons and they should link with schools outside, so that these children can be admitted to properly recognized schools. Every inspector general and superintendent has the capacity to do this."

"You are saying that most prisons do not have child centers?"

"Yes. I don't think anyone has, or at least most do not

have, a nursery school. I will be happily surprised to hear of a single one. The children are the victims of the crime through no fault of their own. Every jail needs a play and education center, irrespective of the number of children in the prison. Link up with NGOs and you will see fantastic results almost immediately."

"Are you implying that Tihar is the role model for other jails?" I asked.

"Though Tihar is way ahead of other jails in terms of reforms, even Tihar is not perfect yet. There is yet a lot to do in Tihar. I would be happy to see Tihar with a school for the children outside the prison. Here the government needs to step in. Some of the work done by NGOs should really be taken up and implemented by each state government. The government ought to initiate these reforms themselves. They should have a school just outside the compound, where the children interact with normal children, and at the end of the day, they come back to the prison and spend the evening and night with their mothers. So, I don't claim that Tihar is perfect. What we are doing as NGOs, though creditable, is still far from perfect. If Tihar can spend millions of rupees constructing more prison buildings, can't they spend a few thousand and build a school for the children who are in prison through no fault of their own? Let the children out of prison. It should be designed as a day boarding school. The child should come to the prison only to sleep with his mother. That is what is needed, and this is something the NGOs can't afford. I can't, as an NGO, build a school.

"What NGOs can do," Dr. Bedi continued, "is place the child in a good recognized school once the child is five years old. My organization, India Vision Foundation, has linked up with five schools to admit children who have stayed with their mothers in prison. Like so many schools, these schools have been very good to us. We find sponsors to partially pay for the cost and do fund-raising for the rest. This project comes under our Crime Home Children Project. The child is not only educated while in prison, but we also make certain that the child is admitted into a residential school that provides for his lodging, boarding, education, and general welfare. In fact, during vacations we take the child back to prison to bond with his mother. Once a month, or once in two months, the child meets with his mother."

"In other states, there are mothers in prison who have not seen their children for months, even years, once the child has left the prison and been admitted to a government-run institution," I said.

"That is the fault of the prison. That is also the fault of the orphanage. They should send the children to their mothers."

"But shouldn't this provision be mandatory? Shouldn't there be a law that makes it compulsory for a mother and child to see each other at least a given number of times in a year?" I asked.

"Absolutely, and that is exactly what I have been saying. All this is in the hands of the prison administration and the Social Welfare Department. This is nothing but an absence of coordination. Can you see the callousness? What is the Social Welfare Department doing? Why should it not ensure that the children and mothers meet regularly? It is their job to inquire when the child has last seen his mother. The person in charge of the orphanage should be monitoring this. You see, Ruzbeh, there are innumerable provisions and rules, but unless there is a human touch, human concern, human compassion, you will keep finding cases where a mother is languishing in prison, dying to see her children, but nobody cares about her plight or the child's misery. Even if there are rules, are the heads of departments held accountable?"

Seeking Justice

"What do you say about the backlog of cases?" I inquired.

"We need special courts, more courts. Without more courts, you will not be able to handle the backlog. Or we could also give incentives to judges who move cases. That should become a criterion for promotion. But our present criterion for promotion is just seniority. Seniority comes even before performance. Another important thing is to make legal amendments to criminal laws to cut down on argument time. The problem with that is that the moment you touch any law, it hurts some vested interest. Then you have a huge strike. Even for civil procedure there was a huge strike. The Supreme Court intervened to protect it. So now you see how every little thing goes to the Supreme Court. Unless this amendment is made, you will have long adjournments; you will have long-winded arguments; and you will have delayed dates. All this suits the criminal world."

"And you have people languishing in jails," I added.

"Yes. You must have seen them languishing. The common man is seeking justice—most of them anyway. But instead of paving fast tracks for justice, the system now digs up existing lanes to create further jams and erects speed breakers. The only way to go about this is to open more channels and then remove the speed breakers."

"There are many mothers who, along with their children, have been languishing in jail awaiting trial for five or six years."

"Approach the Human Rights Commission. Why shouldn't the Human Rights Commission take action? Simple. Finished. Summon the superintendent. Summon the magistrate. The Human Rights Commission has the capacity to do all this and more. Even the local district administration could take action," said Dr. Bedi.

"Why are the lawyers representing these poor people not taking the initiative?"

"Very simple. They get nothing out of it. They get nothing out of it, thus the inaction. The rich clients pay well and the poor clients pay little. There is no incentive to do anything for the poor person. By expediting the judiciary, whom does it suit? Who benefits by speeding up matters in the court of law? That is where the problem starts. The victim has no lawyers. The victim has only the government. The victim is represented by the state government and the state government is crowded. Look at the number of cases the government's prosecutor is handling. Therefore, there is actually no one for the victim. But for the accused there is a lawyer. The accused has the right to a defense. The victim does not have the right to have an expeditious judiciary. The accused has a right to an expeditious trial, but the victim does not have the right to an expeditious decision. Everything works against the victim."

"The victim can appeal to the Human Rights Commission to take a look at his or her case," I said.

"Both the victim and the criminal can appeal! So many times the criminal is innocent. He or she can write to the Human Rights Commission for an early decision. Then the problem is that somebody at all levels has to respond. There are many layers of responsibility, and all of them have to function efficiently for justice to prevail," Dr. Bedi explained.

"Do you really think the Human Rights Commission will listen to every appeal that comes to them?"

"Yes."

"And the Commission will go from prison to prison, addressing individual issues?"

"Yes. It only needs somebody to follow up on the complaint."

"What is your opinion on penal reform taking place in our country?" I asked.

"What penal reform? A program here and a program there is not penal reform. But, unless we do a 180-degree turn, no real good is going to come about."

"You mean like the 180-degree turn you initiated in Tihar?"

"Yes. It was an upside-down change. Cosmetic programs will not help."

"How outdated is our legal system?"

"As old as 1894."

"You mean we are still following laws laid down in the nineteenth century? Nothing has been done to remedy this situation?" I asked incredulously.

"No. As a country, we have not seen any serious major reform in the legal system. No real substantial transformation. Why are you not eating anything?"

It took me a few seconds to shift gears from legal reforms to spicy grams. By then Dr. Bedi had answered a call and given instructions for a household chore to be completed. I wondered how much time it would have taken her to quell the communal riots in Gujarat. Not much, I concluded.

Ordinary Citizens *Can* Make a Difference

"The visiting rooms where the inmates visit with family and friends are pathetic—dark and dismal. Can't something be done to make the visitors' room more humane and homey?" I asked.

"Ruzbeh, somebody should be concerned about this. I am of the firm belief that there is nobody in a better position for concern than the government—those in charge of the prisons and those who are working there. But is creating congenial visiting rooms in prisons a concern for the government or politicians? Is this an issue for a politician? It is not. You see, the price of grain is a political issue. The price of power is a political issue. Even water is a political issue," Dr. Bedi answered.

"God is a political issue," I commented.

"Exactly, but these prisoners are not a political issue. So where do we land? Back in the backyard. Unless an issue becomes a political issue, it doesn't get addressed. Then we come to the next question: if providing humane facilities is not a political issue, then is it an official issue? The answer, once again, is negative. Anything that is not a political issue automatically ceases to be an official issue. Nobody cares."

"So we are back to square one—and to the importance of concerned citizens and NGOs in restoring the lives of the underprivileged and those in shelters," I stated.

"Ordinary citizens can make a world of difference in bettering the lives of the underprivileged. Ordinary citizens, in an organized way, become NGOs. I believe a single citizen is also an NGO. There are many retired people who come to the prison to teach. They are all individuals, playing the role of NGOs."

"But tell me one thing. All of us, every concerned individual, are at the mercy of the inspector general for gaining access into the prison. The point is that if the inspector general does not want the lives of the inmates to get better or has something to hide, then the process of reform halts. How does one make sure that this does not happen?" I asked.

"I do believe that permission to enter the prison should lie in the hands of the inspector general. Why should permission be denied to competent individuals and NGOs? The inspector general is responsible not only for security but also for bettering the lives of those in his care. It finally comes down to the administrator. You have to give him the power of discretion, and he must have a right to say no. I know the answer is often no, when it should be yes."

"Shouldn't there be a procedure that allows concerned individuals and NGOs to serve the inmates, some procedure that is beyond the whim and prejudice of the inspector general in charge?"

"Yes, but there is often a gross misuse by the public also. Tomorrow you might see an excited crowd waving banners of all sorts, marching and shouting slogans, 'Let me in! I must go inside!' So, the inspector general should have the last word. He must have the courage to say no, but then again, he must also use his discretion for the larger good. The inspector general should use his options to make the lives of the inmates more conducive to reform," Dr. Bedi explained.

"Every state has its own jail manual that is used or abused, as per the discretion of those in charge. Why can't there be one standard jail manual for all the prisons—one set of laws and living conditions?" I asked.

"Each state has its own manual. If the states are mishandling their responsibility, this should be brought to light through the Human Rights Commission."

"What steps should be implemented to ensure that a child living in prison will not be scarred for life?"

"First of all, every child must have a normal childhood. That means nursery, health care, cleanliness, clothing, schooling, caring teachers, good company, and environment—all this combined will make a world of difference to the child's psyche. Where women are concerned, vocational training, education, empowerment, legal aid and legal education, clothing, food, and pocket money are all a must."

"When you talk about legal aid, I assume it is mandatory for every prisoner, however poor, to be provided with a lawyer?" I asked.

"Yes, that is mandatory under the Legal Service Act."

"But there are innumerable complaints about these appointed lawyers."

"That may be the case, but magistrates are supposed to be inspecting the prisons, and these are the questions that the magistrates need to be asking. Instead of looking only at the quality of the food, he should also ask the prisoners, 'Who is your lawyer and how good is your lawyer?' He should ask the inmate, 'How many times has your lawyer visited you? Is your lawyer doing his or her job efficiently?'"

"Do you really think that the magistrates are doing all this? Forget about asking the inmates. Do you really believe that they are even visiting the prisons on a regular basis?" I asked.

"Some magistrates are doing their jobs and some don't care at all. It finally comes down to the individual and how well he or she is doing the job."

"How can a prisoner protect and exercise her legal rights?"

"Only through legal knowledge. Does she even know what her rights are? That is what the prison system should first concentrate on. Educate the prisoner. She must be made aware of what is her right and what is not. Often, the staff themselves don't know. What did we do in Tihar? We called in two or three legal-aid groups. They taught the women about their legal rights and about the legal procedure. They got a legal education.

"The moment they knew what was what," continued Dr. Bedi, "they could tell their lawyers, 'This is what I want.' Things began to move immediately after that. Educating them means empowering them. Unfortunately for the prison authorities, ignorance is bliss. It is so much easier to keep prisoners ignorant about their rights. Then we don't have to face the challenge of their growth and change. The moment you bring in NGOs (and concerned professionals), there is added homework for the prison authorities. If they want to do the homework, they will allow NGOs. But if they don't want the added responsibility and are not doing their homework, they won't allow them. It's just like state politics. If you educate the public, then they will hold you accountable and start asking you questions. So the politician thinks it's in his best interest to keep you ignorant, illiterate, and impoverished."

"Other than India, do any other countries allow mother and child to live in the prison?" I inquired.

"Maybe, but not like we have it in India. They allow nursing babies to be with their mothers for a while. The mother may be paroled if the child is nursing, but she isn't allowed to keep her children until they become five years of age. I prefer our Indian way. Some of these women really do need to be in prison. You can't just ignore the fact that some of them are convicted terrorists or are involved in narcotics and murder. There also has to be an element of punishment in the system. But the children should not suffer.

"The important thing," continued Dr. Bedi, "is that there should be a balance in the concept of punishment and freedom. There are people who do not know how to appreciate and be accountable for that freedom. Such people need to be in jail. But I am of the opinion that the mother should keep her child in the prison. That provides a sense of emotional security for the child. It is also a major consolation for the mother, knowing that her child is safe with her, at least for five years. However, if there is no infrastructure, then it is very bad."

"Isn't that happening, no infrastructure?"

"Yes. That is what is generally happening and it is very sad and wrong. Either the government should provide the infrastructure or withdraw permission to keep the child.

But the truth of the situation is, where does the child go? The child still needs the mother. Often, the father is irresponsible and is a greater threat to the child's security than prison. Most of these alcoholic fathers are incestuous, so ironically, the child is safer with the mother in prison than with family and society."

"Shouldn't there be some provision to separate the child from hardcore criminals?"

"Yes, they should separate mothers and children from hardened criminals. New prison construction should keep this aspect in mind and provide separate cells for mothers with their children."

"For that, you need somebody with concern and vision," I said.

"Yes, and we once again come to individual responsibility and accountability. This prison was envisioned and planned carefully. Right after taking over as inspector general of Tihar, I was asked to approve plans for the new prison. I did not see provisions for a separate cell for mothers with children. I did not approve the drawings. It was the last stage. They just needed a signature. I refused. 'Where are the programs? Where is the nursery school? Where is the vocational-training room?' I asked. They said, 'No need for them.' I said, 'Until all these provisions are made in the plans, you will not get a signature from me.' They told me everything would be delayed, but I said, 'That does not matter; what about the hundreds of years the prison will serve people and the thousands of people who will live in it?' I insisted on a reformative building. It took another six months before I approved the plans."

I stood up to leave. I shook her hand. Before leaving, I asked her opinion about the future of the mothers and children in Indian prisons.

"We can't just have bureaucrats. We need activist officials.

As I have said many times, it all boils down to the individual. If you as an individual want to bring about a positive change, then nothing can stop you. If all those in charge of prisons or working within the prisons want to better the lives of mothers and children in prisons, then all that is required is honest intention. Individual responsibility can move mountains."

about the author

Ruzbeh Nari Bharucha began his writing career in his final year of college by editing and publishing the magazine *Venture*. In 1992, he was appointed associate editor, and two years later, chief editor of the first weekly newspaper in Pune, India. He later joined *Indian Express* as the executive editor of the Business Publication Division. His articles have been featured in various publications, including *Times of India*.

Mr. Bharucha is the author of *The Last Marathon*, *Devi's Emerald*, and *Rest in Pieces*. He is currently at work on a documentary about the re-allocation of one of the biggest slums in the world, the Yamuna Pushta, and a book about leprosy.

The Himalayan Institute

The main building of the Institute headquarters near Honesdale, Pennsylvania

Founded in 1971 by Swami Rama, the Himalayan Institute has been dedicated to helping people grow physically, mentally, and spiritually by combining the best knowledge of both the East and the West.

Our international headquarters is located on a beautiful 400-acre campus in the rolling hills of the Pocono Mountains of northeastern Pennsylvania. The atmosphere here is one to foster growth, increase inner awareness, and promote calm. Our grounds provide a wonderfully peaceful and healthy setting for our seminars and extended programs. Students from all over the world join us here to attend programs in such diverse areas as hatha yoga, meditation, stress reduction, ayurveda, nutrition, Eastern philosophy, psychology, and other subjects. Whether the programs are for weekend meditation retreats, week-long seminars on spirituality, months-long residential programs, or holistic health services, the attempt here is to provide an environment of gentle inner progress. We invite you to join with us in the ongoing process of personal growth and development.

The Institute is a nonprofit organization. Your membership in the Institute helps to support its programs. Please call or write for information on becoming a member.

Programs and Services include:

- Weekend or extended seminars and workshops
- Meditation retreats and advanced meditation instruction
- Hatha yoga teachers training
- Residential programs for self-development
- Holistic health services and pancha karma at the Institute's Center for Health and Healing
- Spiritual excursions
- Varcho Veda® herbal products
- Himalayan Institute Press
- *Yoga + Joyful Living* magazine
- Sanskrit correspondence course

The Himalayan Institute also has a long legacy of global humanitarian effort in addition to its dedication to personal self-transformation. In recent decades the Institute has been instrumental in a number of projects in India, including the Himalayan Institute Hospital Trust, earthquake relief, the Himalayan Institute Indian Chapter, schools, a Sanskrit college, and the work of India Vision Foundation in prison reform.

If you would like to support the global humanitarian projects of the Himalayan Institute or would like a *Quarterly Guide to Programs and Other Offerings,* which is free within the USA, or would like any further information, contact us at 1-800-822-4547 or 570-253-5551, write to the Himalayan Institute, 952 Bethany Turnpike, Honesdale, PA 18431, USA, or visit our website at www.HimalayanInstitute.org.

Himalayan Institute Press

The Himalayan Institute Press has long been regarded as the resource for holistic living. We publish dozens of titles, as well as audio and video tapes that offer practical methods for living harmoniously and achieving inner balance. Our approach addresses the whole person-body, mind, and spirit-integrating the latest scientific knowledge with ancient healing and self-development techniques.

As such, we offer a wide array of titles on physical and psychological health and well-being, spiritual growth through meditation and other yogic practices, as well as translations of yogic scriptures.

Our yoga accessories include the Japa Kit for meditation practice and the Neti Pot™, the ideal tool for sinus and allergy sufferers. Our Varcho Veda® line of quality herbal extracts is now available to enhance balanced health and well-being.

Subscriptions are available to a bimonthly magazine, *Yoga+ Joyful Living,* which offers thought-provoking articles on all aspects of meditation and yoga, including yoga's sister science, ayurveda.

For a free catalog, call 800-822-4547 or 570-253-5551, e-mail hibooks@HimalayanInstitute.org, fax 570-647-1552, write to the Himalayan Institute Press, 630 Main St., Suite 350, Honesdale, PA 18431, USA, or visit our website at www.HimalayanInstitute.org.